21st Century Jewelry

THE BEST OF THE 500 SERIES

21ST CENTURY JEWELRY

THE BEST OF THE 500 SERIES

MARTHE LE VAN

LARK
CRAFTS

An Imprint of Sterling Publishing Co., Inc.
New York

WWW.LARKCRAFTS.COM

CONTENT TEAM LEADER
Ray Hemachandra

EDITOR
Julie Hale

EDITORIAL ASSISTANCE
Dawn Dillingham, Abby Haffelt

ART DIRECTOR
Carol Morse Barnao

COVER DESIGNER
Scott Russo

FRONT COVER
Todd Reed
Circular Rose-Cut Brooch, 2006

TITLE PAGE
Nina Basharova
Rock Candy Rings, 2006

OPPOSITE
Jiang Mei-Fang
A Trip for Packing, 2005

Library of Congress Cataloging-in-Publication Data

Le Van, Marthe
21st Century Jewelry : The Best of the 500 Series. -- First Edition.
    pages cm
  ISBN 978-1-60059-521-9 (hc-trade cloth : alk. paper)
  1. Jewelry--History--21st century. I. Le Van, Marthe, editor. II. Title: Twenty-
first Century Jewelry.
  NK7310.5.A15 2011
  739.2709'0511--dc22

                                    2010048613

10 9 8 7 6 5 4 3 2 1

First Edition

Published by Lark Crafts, An Imprint of
Sterling Publishing Co., Inc.
387 Park Avenue South, New York, NY 10016

Text © 2011, Lark Crafts, an Imprint of Sterling Publishing Co., Inc.
Photography © 2011, Artist/Photographer

Distributed in Canada by Sterling Publishing,
c/o Canadian Manda Group, 165 Dufferin Street
Toronto, Ontario, Canada M6K 3H6

Distributed in the United Kingdom by GMC Distribution Services,
Castle Place, 166 High Street, Lewes, East Sussex, England BN7 1XU

Distributed in Australia by Capricorn Link (Australia) Pty Ltd.,
P.O. Box 704, Windsor, NSW 2756 Australia

If you have questions or comments about this book, please contact:
Lark Crafts
67 Broadway
Asheville, NC 28801
828-253-0467

Manufactured in China

ISBN 13: 978-1-60059-521-9

For information about custom editions, special sales, and premium and corporate purchases, please contact the Sterling Special Sales Department at 800-805-5489 or specialsales@sterlingpub.com.

For information about desk and examination copies available to college and university professors, requests must be submitted to academic@larkbooks.com. Our complete policy can be found at www.larkcrafts.com.

Contents

Foreword 6

Introductions: Leading Voices 7

The Jewelry 12

The Jurors 404

Acknowledgments 415

Contributing Artists 420

Foreword

It was risky to **drive through a hurricane** to jury my first jewelry collection. Perilous road and weather conditions, not to mention a white-knuckled assistant, made me question the decision mile after mile. But the payoff at the end of this foolish journey would change my life forever.

I had traveled to meet Robert Ebendorf, one of America's most influential art jewelers. Over the next three days, from sun up to well past dark, we looked at thousands of jewelry slides. Bob introduced me to the artists and the art form that would **inspire my professional life**. My reckless behavior led to incredible fortune, and the wild ride continues to this day.

Out of that fateful storm came *1000 Rings*, one of the most **groundbreaking, successful, and influential books** on contemporary jewelry. Nine books followed in the next 10 years, juried by prominent makers, teachers, gallery owners, writers, and curators. *21st Century Jewelry* showcases the **finest pieces from these collections** in one very special edition.

JANE DODD
Rabbit Leuchterweibchen Brooch | 2007

How is it special? Well for starters, 80 jewelers juried the collection. Each was given **free rein** to choose their favorite pieces out of any "500" jewelry book, and they had to tell us about each choice. What makes the piece a standout? How does it speak to them? What are its outstanding qualities? Their selections and remarks provide a **unique context** for this decade of jewelry making and **fantastic insight** into the eye, mind, and heart of the makers.

To introduce the book, we turned to a panel of international experts. These collectors, teachers, curators, and gallery owners are **essential to the vitality and advancement** of contemporary jewelry. We asked them to describe the past 10 years in jewelry and to predict what exciting developments may be in store for the next decade, and they responded with lively and diverse viewpoints.

One-of-a-kind jewelry, designed and created by **passionate artists**, is a fascinating art form that can be appreciated on a variety of levels. Contemporary jewelry brings together aesthetics, technique, tradition, identity, community, commentary, beauty, and worth. It asserts its meanings in an exceptional way—by being worn.

Lovers of art and design introduced to contemporary jewelry will discover a dynamic, enthralling, and endlessly evolving field. Equal parts **art and science, imagination and engineering, grace and grit**, jewelry making attracts individualists committed to originality, improvement, and growth.

Fortunately, there's no need for you to drive through a hurricane to become acquainted with this **magnificent creative community**. This thorough collection encapsulates 10 years of books featuring work by leading jewelry artists across the globe.

MARTHE LE VAN
Editor and Curator
Asheville, North Carolina

Introductions: Leading Voices

Without doubt, the end of the 20th century witnessed the breakdown of many preconceptions—What is jewelry? What materials can be used? What about wearability? Every aspect of the notion of jewelry was questioned, often through a statement of negation.

However, in the first decade of the new century, I have noticed a tendency to move forward from obligatory attempts to make jewelry a "revolutionary, provocative declaration." It seems to me that, in the past few years, it's finally been taken for granted that jewelry can be almost anything. It has proved to be a form of art like any other.

Thus, having "gained" this freedom of expression, jewelers are concentrating again on forms, finesse of details, beauty, and experimentation, both technical and stylistic.

I look forward to seeing where this tendency will lead us, in the hands of fresh artists and with the aid of new technologies. I don't know if all of this is truly happening, but at least this is what I wish to see.

After all, jewelry contains JOY in its name (from Latin *jocus* and Old French *joule*—"jest" or "plaything"), and I believe that must be its function.

GIOVANNI CORVAJA

Brooch | 2000

GIOVANNI CORVAJA
Goldsmith and Teacher
Todi, Italy

The first decade of the 21st century **shattered our security**—empowering terrorists to coordinate airplane-crashing mass murders on U.S. soil, magnifying and spreading financial viruses at reaction-defying pace, broadcasting web-based political extremism, and reducing dialogue to two-word tweets. At the same time, the wrenching chaos opened minds, democratized expression, stimulated creativity, blurred distinctions, and encouraged generosity—a perfect moment for artists, particularly artists making jewelry, to reexamine the past and go into the future.

As the centuries changed, master jeweler Gijs Bakker **refreshed the conceptual dialogue** through his newly founded design collaborative "Chi ha paura…?" or "Who is afraid (of contemporary jewelry)…?" Bakker captured the decade's manic mood swings in *The Cry* (2010), referencing Edvard Munch's 1893 painting of a deathbed mask exuding horror and excitement amidst a turbulent landscape. Bakker licensed a computer program to design *The Cry*, a three-dimensional metal skull brooch with 50 tiny diamonds. It depicts an athlete at peak exertion spewing adrenaline-fueled energy and pain from his wide-open mouth.

The first decade also witnessed Berlin jewelry artist Svenja John add extruded polycarbonate ring material—the same plastic used for chain-mail costumes in *Lord of The Rings*—to her jewelry repertoire, while Alexander Blank combined horror with humor, producing acrylic shield brooches, flower wallpapered tank necklaces, and sculpted futuristic animal-head brooches. The next decade of the 21st century promises other **new materials and computer-directed inventions** with which to design, create, color, build, and fasten jewelry.

Further progress will be made to break down the distinction between artists making jewelry and "Fine Artists." Already, **major barriers** blocking jewelry artists from

SVENJA JOHN
Breath Brooch | 2001

fine art museums **have been felled**: the 2002 acquisition of the Helen Drutt collection by the Museum of Fine Arts, Houston, and the Boston Museum of Fine Arts' acquisition of Daphne Fargo's collection in 2006 (lifting the Boston museum's holdings to the most comprehensive collection of studio jewelry ever assembled).

This decade will see more museums, nonprofit spaces, and Internet platforms for artist jewelry. Mainstream auction houses will offer jewelry made by contemporary artists, bringing transparent pricing and **confirmation of value** to the work. More important contemporary art-jewelry books and catalogues will become available, and major art magazines will review exhibitions of jewelry made by artists. The rethinking and excitement as the world reorients itself during the second decade of the 21st century will jolt creativity and witness jewelry artists claiming their rightful place.

MARI SHAW
Collector
New York and Berlin

ere's how I would describe the last 10 years in jewelry—"Just one word…Plastics." Even if Benjamin Braddock was not listening to Mr. Maguire in the 1969 film *The Graduate*, some contemporary jewelers were. In a time that only defined jewelry as high-karat gold and diamonds, a few trailblazers decided to challenge prevailing attitudes.

The past decade has been a Renaissance of sorts for the use of plastic in all its forms and chemical structures. The jeweler synonymous with the material is Peter Chang. His exuberant forms and scale have brought this lowly material great respect from fellow jewelers, museums, and collectors. A beautiful example will challenge gold and diamonds as far as value is concerned.

American jewelers using plastic have come into their own. Bruce Metcalf and Lisa Gralnick were early proponents. In her *City Flora/City Flotsam* series, Jan Yager incorporated plastic crack-cocaine vials into historically referenced jewelry. Now, plastics appear in many jewelers' design and production—emiko oye refashions toy building blocks, Natalya Pinchuk incorporates commercial plastics into enamel or fiber brooches, and Diane Falkenhagen carves Corian into pillow forms.

Plastic jewelry has been celebrated through major books and exhibitions, yet plastic remains unrecognized as a craft material, per se. The past 10 years have made a forceful statement to the importance of this substance and presented a strong case for its inclusion with glass, clay, fiber, metals, and wood as a significant craft material.

I am most excited by the fearlessness of our makers. Academic metals programs continue to attract intelligent, thoughtful, meticulous students searching for their own voices. This, in itself, is not particularly new, but student attitudes about exploration and their willingness to push the definition and boundary of what constitutes ornamentation is aggressive to say the least. Subjects heretofore unseen in jewelry are viable and sometimes profound.

Almost as exciting is the opportunity these new jewelers present to capture a different breed of wearers. Ornamentation, whether by jewelry, clothing, or body modification, is embraced with enthusiasm by the young. Children sport "cause" bracelets. Adolescents add their own talismans to identify with a tribe. These are all potential new art-jewelry collectors.

Will they embrace the same considerations of today's collectors? Probably not. But the excitement rests in what kind of stamp these new collectors and makers will bring to the ongoing history of jewelry and ornamentation. Can jewelry be more conceptual? We'll see. Will it find new ways and places to be worn on the body? Surely. Will it still engage us as wearers to want to put a little of our private selves on display for all to see? I really hope so.

PETER CHANG
Untitled | 2004

RON PORTER
Collector
Columbia, South Carolina

A notable change over the past 10 years in art jewelry has been the increasing importance of photography and the digital dissemination of images via blogs, websites, and community forums. This **explosion of access** has created a wealth of opportunity and freedom for younger and emerging artists, but it has also encouraged a kind of **"international style"** with a tendency toward plagiarism and a lack of rigor in individual development. There's a proliferation of people experimenting with and producing jewelry, which is wonderful, but it has become difficult to find truly fresh and individual voices among the throng.

I'm excited about the emerging artists and students who, while absorbing and filtering the myriad influences available to them, will also have the energy and discipline to move beyond those influences and develop a **unique and truly personal** visual language.

KATIE SCOTT
Director, Gallery Funaki
Melbourne, Australia

A little more than 10 years ago, I discovered the world of art jewelry and began an ongoing **love affair** with it, so this retrospective has come at an appropriate time for me. The past decade has brought me so much joy. I have learned so much, met so many wonderful, international makers, seen so much exquisite work, and gradually **built a collection** that I am passionate about. Jewelry is a huge part of my life. It has taken a long time, but at last I have found out what rocks my boat.

Those who took a chance by **opening a gallery** at a time when the jewelry we admire and love today had little or no exposure were **true pioneers**, but they will not be around forever. We need people to follow in their footsteps. In the next 10 years, I hope we'll see a new breed of young gallery owners who will become the successors and a fitting tribute to these pioneers.

I hope that the next generation of jewelers will not become too process-driven because of access to new technologies, as this could lead to the work losing integrity. Instead, I would like to see a **loyalty to the value of the handmade**.

Most of all, I look forward to continuing to support this unique area of art by adding to my collection, and discovering and following new makers as well as those who are more established. I hope I never stop **feeling butterflies** when I encounter new work. And to make a few friends along the way would be the icing on the cake!

JO BLOXHAM
Curator and Collector
Manchester, United Kingdom

KARL FRITSCH
Die Tränen von Pandora | 2004

Within the past 10 years, the jewelry field has grown immensely. New books, magazines, videos, and an expanded Internet caused the field to **explode at breakneck speed** with more artists, more images, more information, more adventurous collectors and buyers, and more museums purchasing art jewelry. Even artists from other fields designed jewelry, such as architect Frank Gehry. At the same time, too many important **jewelry departments in academia were closed**, and those losses were painful. Yet, the number of people entering jewelry grew, and the field became larger in its scope of approaches to materials, scale, function, and form.

With its exploration of nontraditional or alternative materials, the "New Jewelry" movement of the 1970s and 1980s had an enormous impact. Since then, all or any materials for jewelry seemed valid, including precious metals and gemstones, found objects, virtual images, and ephemeral substances, such as Naomi Filmer's objects of ice. New materials appeared in the marketplace and therefore in jewelry. Jewelry was not defined by the preciousness of the materials, but rather it took its value from **its ideas, its content, and its form**.

The work of Arline Fisch, especially *Body Ornament* from 1966, inspired the idea of **monumental jewelry**, and within the past decade, there was no holding back. Many pieces verged on being unwearable or were intended to be worn for only a short period of time. My own work has been of a large scale since the late 1960s. *The Cage* body sculpture (116.3 x 61 x 86.4 cm), in the collection of the Muskegon Museum of Art, Muskegon, Michigan, could not be worn in a car and one could not even walk through most doorways with it on, so it was in a category that caused questions about the functionality of jewelry or body sculptures. Within the past decade, there were many

MARJORIE SCHICK
For Want of a Nail | 2001

more works in this category that challenged both the wearer and the viewer to **redefine jewelry**.

Additional recent influences include new technologies, growing interest in **environment-friendly materials, recycling**, the source of mined objects, and economic and political conditions. Narrative jewelry built around a story or concept was not new to the decade, but it continued and expanded in scope. Many jewelers communicated very personal ideas. Such **intimate moments** can be seen in Melanie Bilenker's drawings made with human hair set in resin.

The field will continue to grow, and there will be much exploration and experimentation with new materials and technologies, with scale, with function, and with form. It is possible that there may be a reversal in approach that causes jewelry to **become quieter, more user-conscious, and more subtle**. The rhythms of life ebb and flow, so it will be exciting to watch what happens in the next decade.

MARJORIE SCHICK
Jeweler and Teacher
Pittsburg, Kansas

CESAR LIM
Shield Ring | 2007
6.4 X 2.5 X 3 CM

Aquamarines, tourmaline, diamonds,
18-karat white gold, silver; hand forged,
fabricated, oxidized, textured
PHOTO BY VLAD LAVROVSKY

A stunning photo that not only captures the voluminous effect of the necklace, but has an **energy and movement** of its own. Like a spray of foam from the sea, a **beautifully controlled chaos**. ■ *emiko oye*

SEAININ PASSI
Resin Droplet Neckpiece | 2007
25 X 30 X 20 CM
Polyester resin, mild steel wire,
steel fuse wire; wrapped, soldered, shaped
PHOTO BY RICHARD BOLL PHOTOGRAPHY

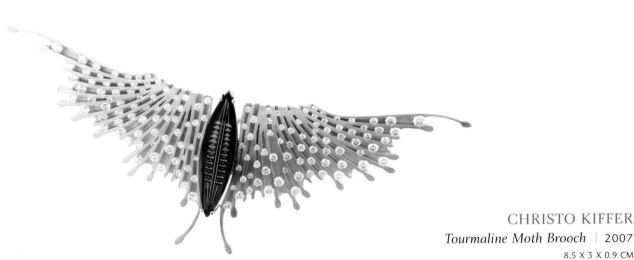

CHRISTO KIFFER
Tourmaline Moth Brooch | 2007
8.5 X 3 X 0.9 CM
Green tourmaline, diamonds,
18-karat yellow gold; hand fabricated
PHOTOS BY ARTIST

I adore this brooch for its intricate diamond-setting technique on the wings, which sets off the intricate cuts in the gem. **Christo is a rare talent, indeed.** The second reason to love this brooch is the gorgeous Munsteiner-cut green tourmaline. The Munsteiners are the world's preeminent gem cutters, and it is always exciting to see how jewelry artists take their art and carry it further. ■ *Cindy Edelstein*

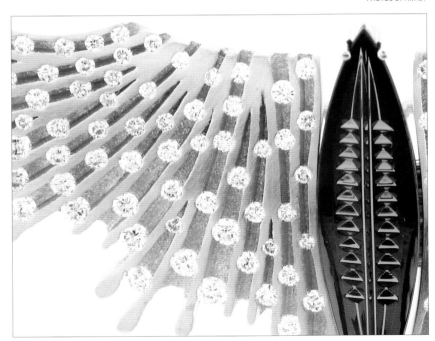

What **amazes** me about these earrings is their size. The photograph makes them seem really large, especially seeing how many separate leaf-like elements make up the interior. I was surprised when I realized they are only an inch square. ■ *Geoffrey D. Giles*

Incredibly tactile earrings.

I want to touch them. ■ *Deborrah Daher*

JACQUELINE RYAN
Untitled | 2002
EACH, 2.6 X 2.6 X 0.8 CM
18-karat gold; hand pierced, forged, soldered
PHOTO BY GIOVANNI CORVAJA

The multiplication of tiny leaf-like elements creates a **rich and sensuous surface** that will reflect light as the wearer moves. The intimate scale gives the earrings a **quiet elegance** that will enhance the wearer. ■ *Arline M. Fisch*

The rough gemstone is **mesmerizing**. You continue to look at the textures as well as the color and the shape. The use of rough diamonds around the stone adds to the texture and color for a very arresting gemstone jewel that **showcases the natural beauty of the gems**.

■ *Cindy Edelstein*

MICHAEL ZOBEL
Brooch/Pendant—Broken Heart | 2008
6.2 X 4.5 X 0.5 CM
Sterling silver, 22-karat gold,
platinum, tourmaline, diamonds
PHOTO BY FRED THOMAS

KLAUS SPIES
Moebius | 2003
2 X 2 X 0.7 CM
18-karat yellow gold, Burmese rubies;
wax carved, cast, channel set
PHOTO BY LARRY SANDERS

SONDRA SHERMAN
Untitled | 2005

9.5 X 2.5 X 2.5 CM

Sterling silver, 18-karat gold,
aquamarine; die formed, pierced,
hand wrought, constructed

PHOTOS BY MARTY DOYLE

Jesse Mathes ignores the distracting issue of wearability and constructs collars that reveal much broader truths about why people wear jewelry. Jewelry creates an identity, whether on an intimate scale like a diamond ring, or just to say, "here I am, come closer only if you dare, my personal space reaches out to a specific boundary beyond which I am veiled in secrecy." ■ *Harriete Estel Berman*

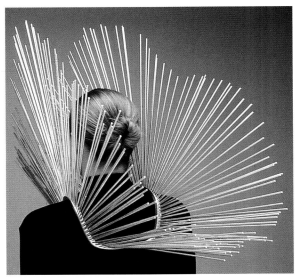

JESSE MATHES
Rebato | 2004
96.5 X 35.6 X 61 CM
Aluminum; tap and die, sanded
PHOTOS BY MICHAEL CAVANAGH AND KEVIN MONTAGUE

Ancestral Memories is a **visceral gift**. It transports me to the sea where I feel small in the face of the pounding tide, yet transformed by the sound of the waves and the smell and taste of the salt air. This ring conveys a sense of **unity, responsibility, and purpose**. ■ *Marthe Le Van*

OWEN MAPP
Ancestral Memories | 2003
10 X 4 CM
Bone; hand carved
PHOTO BY ARTIST

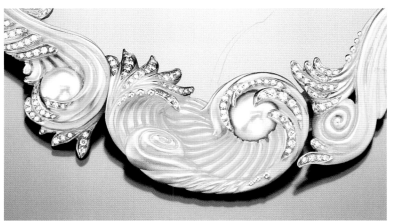

KIM ERIC LILOT
Hokusai Tribute Necklace | 2008
45 CM LONG
18-karat royal yellow and white gold, rosé pearls, diamonds; pavé set, lost wax cast, fabricated
PHOTOS BY HAP SAKWA

The photograph is beautiful
and captures the true
essence of the wearing
experience. I can almost
reach out and touch
the fur, and yet it is so
ephemeral. I know if I
wore it, it would surely lose
its **perfect beauty**, but
that is why I love it.

Deborah Lozier

HEATHER WHITE
Circle Ring: Pet | 2002
6.4 X 6.4 X 2.2 CM
Gold, sterling silver, fur; constructed
PHOTO BY DEAN POWELL

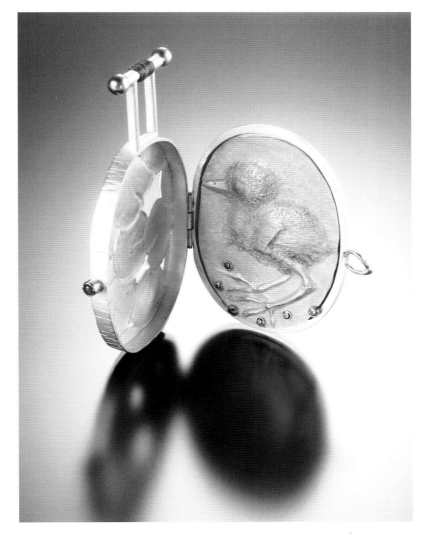

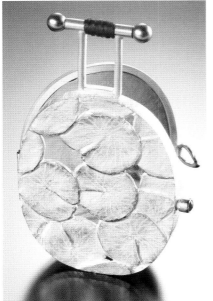

L. KINDLER PRIEST
Baby Lily Trotter | 2005
6.5 X 3.5 X 0.8 CM
Ruby, 14-karat gold, silk thread, pearls,
diamonds; set, repoussé
PHOTOS BY GORDON BERNSTEIN

I have always respected Felieke's world of **unique creatures**. Her jewelry fables are playful, original, and very **easy to fall in love with**. ■ *Hanna Hedman*

FELIEKE VAN DER LEEST
The Grey Lady with the Chicken Legs | 2004
9.5 X 5.5 X 2.5 CM
Textile, rubber, hematite,
store-bought toy; crocheted, knitted
PHOTO BY EDDO HARTMANN

NEL LINSSEN
Untitled | 1986
EACH, 5 X 8 CM IN DIAMETER
Paper, elastic; folded
PHOTO BY PETER BLIEK

Small treasures. So **familiar and personal**.

Hidden messages contained quietly within. ■ *Sim Luttin*

NICOLE JACQUARD
Letters & Notes | 2004–2007
EACH, 3.5 X 2 X 2 CM
Aluminum, nylon cord; photocopied,
transferred, folded
PHOTO BY KATHRYN WANDILL

I am writing this one day after President Obama's announcement of an official end to U.S. military involvement in Iraq, and just over a month since Marcia Macdonald passed into her own peace after her illness with cancer. This brooch she created, far in advance of either of these events, nonetheless encompasses them today, and demonstrates the power of jewelry to resonate on both the intimate and international scale. *Peace* embodies both the strength and the fragility of our bodies, our lives, and the harmony of our world, and it quietly hums with the hope and support that all of these may flourish. Its punctum and gravitas are generously tempered with the whimsy that is perhaps my favorite of all the wonderful things about Marcia's work. ■ *Nisa Blackmon*

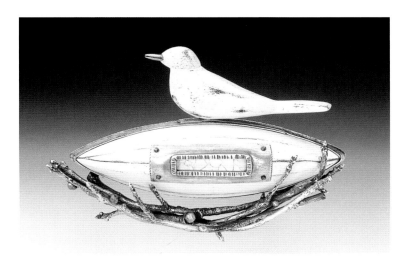

MARCIA A. MACDONALD
Peace | 2003
7.6 X 11.4 X 2.5 CM
Sterling silver, wood, paint,
eggshell, thermoplastic
PHOTO BY HAP SAKWA

To a certain extent, I know the work of Ela Bauer. I've seen some in exhibitions, and I characterize them as works that **breathe life**. Their organic configuration is not gratuitous. It reports to us a subtle world she may want us to discover or rediscover. ■ *Leonor Hipólito*

ELA BAUER
Untitled | 2004
40 X 1 CM
Silicone rubber, pigment, thread;
cast, hand fabricated, sewn
PHOTO BY ARTIST

This is such a strong image, yet it uses such **delicate lines**. ▪ *Thomas Hill*

Enamel reinvented on constructions of wire; delicate and yet very powerful. ▪ *Charon Kransen*

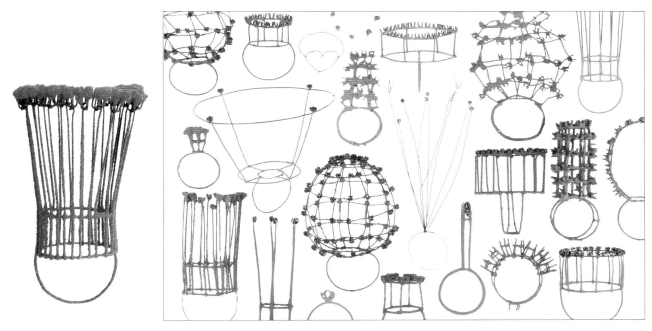

BETTINA DITTLMANN
Ringchen | 2001–2003
0.1 X 2.3 X 2.7 CM TO 7.4 X 6 X 6 CM
Iron wire, garnet, pyrite, enamel;
soldered, bezel set
PHOTOS BY DITTLMANN/JANK

Dittlmann creates a **visual language** all her own. Perhaps not very practical in terms of wearability, but the **inventiveness** in thin steel wire, red enamel, and garnets is exhilarating. ▪ *Mike Holmes*

Impossible pieces brought into this world by Bettina Dittlmann. Hardly wearable, but they **insist on being jewelry**. The texture and the warmth of the color in contrast to the fragility of the line is **compelling**. Unbelievably well done pieces in all remarks. They are rings for imaginary princesses, including me. ▪ *Castello Hansen*

JENNACA LEIGH DAVIES
Paper Pendant | 2006
10 X 8 X 8 CM
Paper, plastic and steel cording; laser cut
PHOTOS BY STEFFEN KNUDSEN ALLEN

Jennaca's *Paper Pendant* has always been an **icon** for me of everything good about modern technology. The **fractal volume** created by systematic cutting of the star shapes combined with her **exquisite color** choice creates an otherworldly blossom. ■ *Rebecca Hannon*

There could have been an **explosion** just before, and what you see is the result—a beautiful object looking like an underwater flower. full of colors and delicate details.

Karin Seufert

Pristine, crisp, tinted acrylic that's laminated, thermoformed, hand carved, and polished, resulting in plastic that looks like glass. Amazing how he does that. *Susan Kasson Sloan*

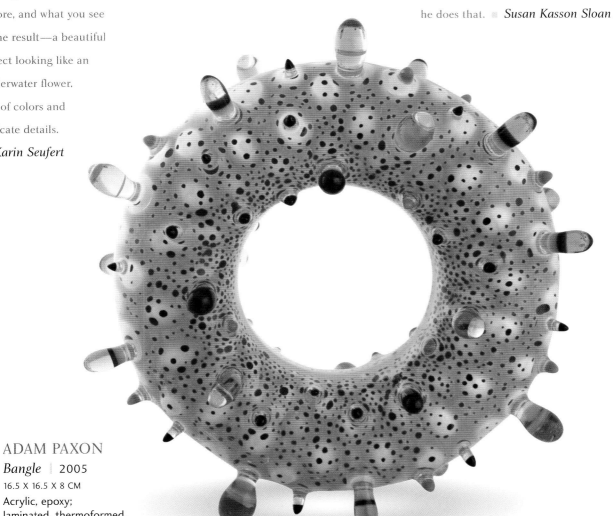

ADAM PAXON
Bangle | 2005
16.5 X 16.5 X 8 CM
Acrylic, epoxy; laminated, thermoformed, hand carved, polished
PHOTO BY PAUL AMBTMAN

Norwegian Soul Brooch appeals to me because of the multiple use of circles within circles to build a layered **symmetry**. The bold **contrast** of black, pearl, and gold against the subtlety of the black coil circles is **stark and complex**, but there is a fun feeling about this brooch. ■ *Linda MacNeil*

PAMELA RITCHIE
Norwegian Soul Brooch | 2007
4.8 X 4.8 X 1.2 CM
Sterling silver, 18-karat gold, pearls
PHOTO BY PERRY JACKSON

DAHLIA KANNER
Open Pocket Ears | 1999
EACH, 4 X 2.4 X 0.6 CM
Sterling silver, silver, pearls,
garnet, patina; cast
PHOTO BY MARK JOHNSTON

This massive necklace (not to be unnoticed) persuades by its **authenticity** and **pureness**, reflecting the personality of the artist. ■ *Claude Schmitz*

PAULA CRESPO
Untitled | 1994
18 X 3 CM
Silver; hand fabricated, oxidized
PHOTO BY JOAO CARVALHO DE SOUSA

I am interested in forms that recall anatomy. These remind me of a study of the lungs' morphology and breath and are successful in their **lightness** and **simplicity**. ■ *Leonor Hipólito*

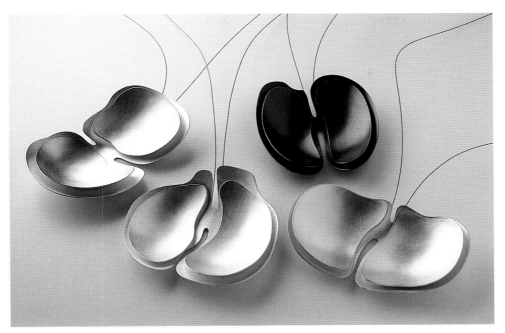

LESLIE MATTHEWS
Untitled | 2002
AVERAGE, 6 X 5 X 2 CM
Sterling silver, steel cable; oxidized
PHOTO BY GRANT HANCOCK

TOMOYO HIRAIWA
Peace Circle I | 2009
12 X 5 CM
Silver; oxidized
PHOTO BY YOSHITAKA UCHIDA

CHRIS IRICK

Passage | 2002

7.5 X 6 X 6 CM

Sterling silver; fabricated,
die formed, soldered, pierced

PHOTOS BY ARTIST
COURTESY OF MUNSON-WILLIAMS-PROCTOR
ARTS INSTITUTE MUSEUM OF ART, UTICA, NEW YORK

I respond to the **organic form** of this ring in contrast to its mechanics. I also love the variation in the ring when it sits closed on the finger and when it is open. The hammered texture creates a **beautiful surface** revealing the forming process. ■ *Sue Amendolara*

This was the first piece that came to mind when asked to pick favorites from the "500" series. A beautiful combination of form and movement. **I love rings you can play with while wearing**. Fantastic use of the collapsible cup idea. ■ *Chris Irick*

PATTY L. COKUS
Articulated Frusta: Phonograph Ring | 2002
5 X 4.4 X 4.4 CM (EXTENDED);
3.8 X 3.8 X 4.4 CM (COLLAPSED)
Sterling silver, black patina, 14-karat yellow gold; fabricated
PHOTOS BY ARTIST

JANE ADAM
Spiral Bangles | 1999
AVERAGE, 5 X 6 X 6 CM
Aluminum, dye; anodized, crazed
PHOTO BY JOËL DEGEN

Normally I find anodized aluminum too garish, but Jane Adam is able to tame the material and bring such a beautiful and painterly surface to her bracelets. ◾ *Donald Friedlich*

The colors and textures are so rich, enveloping the perfect, simple form. Wonderful to look at and easy to visualize on my arm. I can feel their warmth and comfort lifting off the page. ◾ *Deborah Lozier*

These earrings look like **big eyes** that have an **open view** to the world outside. ■ *Birgit Laken*

BEATE KLOCKMANN
Apple Earrings | 2006
EACH, 5.5 X 2.5 X 2.5 CM
14-karat gold, enamel, copper, silver; niello
PHOTO BY ARTIST

Adding the touch of an **elegant** white diamond to the **rough** nature of the steel results in a simple, yet compelling bracelet.

— *Gurhan Orhan*

PEG FETTER

Tension Bracelet with Diamond | 2003

5 X 8 X 1 CM

Steel, 14-karat gold, diamond; forged, fabricated, tube set, heat beaded, heat oxidized, waxed

PHOTO BY DON CASPER

The scale, material, and structure of the gold surface are **refined** and **timeless**. Here, the order of the construction meets the free morphology of the gold plates. Holes grant a mysterious character to this jewelry. ▪ *Pavel Herynek*

STEFANO MARCHETTI
Untitled | 1995
2.5 X 2.5 X 1.5 CM
Gold; mokume gane, parquetry
PHOTO BY ROBERTO SORDI

Mysterious beauty.
▪ *Deborrah Daher*

MIWHA OH
Power of Unknown | 1997
2.5 X 3.8 X 0.6 CM
Steel, 20-karat gold; cast, soldered
PHOTO BY MYUNG-WOOK HUH, STUDIO MUNCH

RALLOU KATSARI
Third Pass | 2006
7.5 X 5 X 4 CM
Silver, pigment; oxidized, hammered
PHOTO BY ARTIST

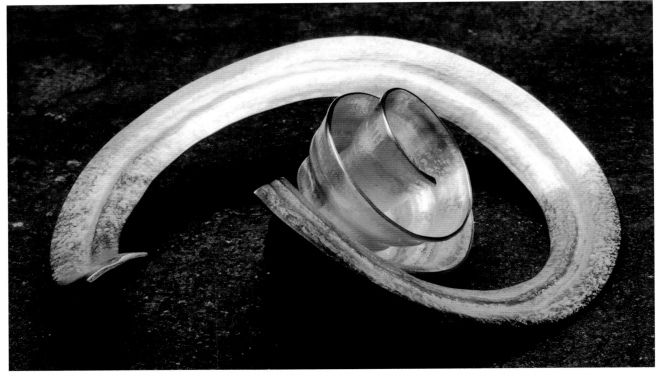

CATHERINE CLARK GILBERTSON
Spiral Earpiece | 2005

2.6 X 5.7 CM

18-karat gold; chased, repoussé

PHOTOS BY TOM MCINVAILLE

Beautiful and strong. I love the
directness of the design and the flow
of the metal. ■ *Deborrah Daher*

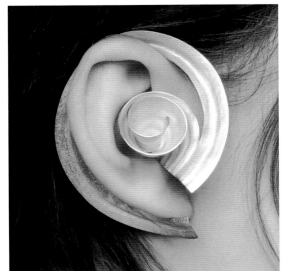

I love the **whimsy** of this piece, and the manner in which all of its elements describe not only the **shape** of "fold," but also the **action** of folding itself.

■ *George Sawyer*

ALAN REVERE
Fold | 2003
5.7 X 2.5 X 3.2 CM
18-karat yellow gold, 14-karat red gold,
platinum, diamonds; corrugated, fabricated

PHOTO BY BARRY BLAU

GINA PANKOWSKI
Tighra #3 | 2002
8.5 X 8.5 X 2 CM
18-karat gold; cast, hand fabricated
PHOTO BY DOUGLAS YAPLE

The repetition of conical forms hints at the macroscopic worlds revealed when one examines the detailed structures found in nature. This piece comes alive when worn, referring to the historical tradition of *en tremblant* jewelry or "tremblers." Though made with precious gold, the brooch escapes any pretension of opulence. It is elegant and complex in its seeming simplicity.

■ *Wendy McAllister*

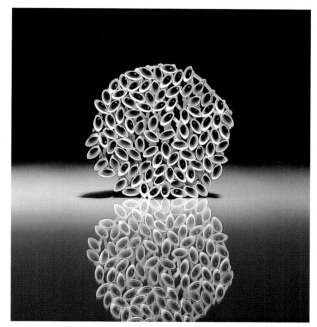

JACQUELINE RYAN
Brooch | 1999
6 CM IN DIAMETER
18-karat gold, enamel
PHOTO BY GIOVANNI CORVAJA

A perfect design.
■ *Tom Munsteiner*

Jacqueline Ryan's brooch brings to mind clusters of seeds, eggs, or flowers. The repetitive elements allude to an ordered system, but tumble back into chaos, as if everything is in flux. Whenever I see Ryan's pieces, I study the intricate connections between elements and find comfort in her production of multiples that are almost identical, yet each distinct.

■ *Cappy Counard*

TOM MUNSTEINER
Ring: Magic Eye | 2008
2.9 X 3 X 1 CM
Morganite, 18-karat yellow gold
PHOTO BY ARTIST

The delicate method of construction, the spotless skin, and the beautiful saturated yellow color turn these **deceptively beautiful**, geometric flowers into alluring Venus Fly Traps. Just plain vicious! ■ *Klaus Burgel*

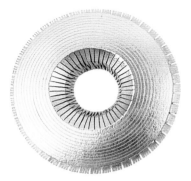 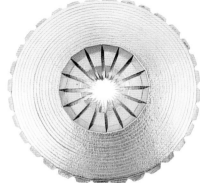 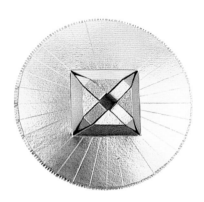

LISA GRALNICK
Three Brooches | 2002
1.9 X 7 TO 8.3 CM IN DIAMETER
18-karat gold; fabricated
PHOTO BY ARTIST

Lisa's technical capabilities are unreal. This, combined with a commitment to **conceptual and formal rigor**, allows her work to move beyond the merely formal to the **magical**. ■ *Seth Papac*

Light, colorful, and fun…how can I not fall in love with these brooches?

All parts are in balance—the precious with the discarded, the controlled form with the implicit lightness of coexisting parts, the traditional and the alternative. ■ *Natalya Pinchuk*

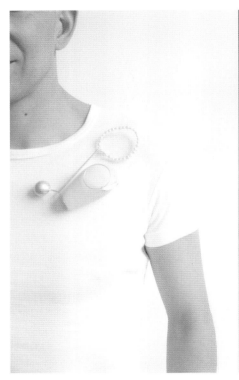 

JANTJE FLEISCHHUT
Sateliten 2 Series: Weisses | 2003
4 X 5 X 9 CM
Found plastic, epoxy, fiberglass,
silver, pearls, found rubber, citrine
PHOTOS BY ARTIST

The ubiquitous price tags of today's consumer society are disguised in this **elegant** brooch. Suspended by a geometric, gold-plated frame, the translucent tags overlap to create **captivating** shapes. I quietly question, "What is value?"

◼ *Anastasia Azure*

CHRISTEL VAN DER LAAN
Priceless Brooch | 2006
6.3 X 6.3 X 0.7 CM
Gold-plated sterling silver,
polypropylene price tags
PHOTO BY ROBERT FRITH

One of my favorite
quotes by Mies van
der Rohe sums up
Claude's work for me:
"Less is More."
■ *Michael Good*

CLAUDE CHAVENT
Cage | 2004
6.7 X 5.5 X 0.5 CM
Platinum, 18-karat gold;
trompe l'oeil
PHOTO BY ARTIST

What can I say, I love this piece. **What is precious or valuable?** I think this is incredibly awesome and probably will look so good on.

■ *Todd Reed*

JENNIFER KELLOGG
Diamond Necklace | 2001
46 X 2 CM
Sterling silver, enamel
PHOTO BY LUIS ERNESTO SANTANA

A heart, a cross, an arrow, a skull, Mickey Mouse, the Klu Klux Klan. I see these things in this **magnificent, simple** brooch. But there are probably more I have not discovered yet.

■ *Felieke van der Leest*

A most poignant and concise piece. It is at once **iconic, funny**, and **chilling**. Perhaps the most pointed piece of jewelry of the 20th century.

■ *Lisa and Scott Cylinder*

OTTO KÜNZLI
Oh, Say! | 1991
9 X 9 X 0.6 CM
Gold
PHOTO BY ARTIST

The idea, brooch, and presentation combine **triumphantly.** The 'souvenir' and the 'postcard' are fundamental to most travelers' experiences of iconic landmarks. The simplicity of the form and the seemingly nonchalant position of the brooch image speak volumes about tourist colonization and its "souvenir-ing"… ■ *Peter Deckers*

CATHELIJNE ENGELKES
Plated Postcard Cities | 2002
BROOCH, 2 X 1 CM;
DISPLAY, 12.2 X 16.5 X 3.5 CM
Postcards, box, silver, gold; plated
PHOTO BY TED NOTEN

The most interesting aspects to me are that the ring is not in direct connection with the body, but with a clothing item. It is not visible and gives the impression that it is stuck by accident in the heel sole. This consideration is the beginning of a story. **Who did the ring belong to? In what circumstance was it lost and where?** ▪ *Fabrizio Tridenti*

What is a ring?

Round, precious, sparkling? But this one is not worn on the finger but on the sole of a shoe. Gisbert Stach makes **mischief** with the entire notion of a ring and recaptures the prankishness of childhood. ▪ *Mary Hallam Pearse*

GISBERT STACH
Firestep | 1994
RING, 2.4 X 2.4 X .7 CM
18-karat gold, flints, shoes; embedded
PHOTO BY ARTIST

OTTO KÜNZLI
Faceless | 1993
3.5 X 3.5 X 0.8 CM
Gold; cast
PHOTO BY ARTIST

Künzli is a master of **simplicity**.
▪ *Charlotte De Syllas*

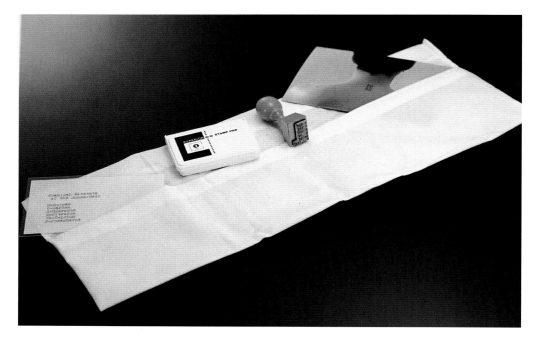

CATHELIJNE ENGELKES
*The Chemical Elements of a
Human Body* | 2003
DISPLAY, 20 X 54 CM; STAMP, 2.6 X 1.7 CM
Stamp, photo indication, ink,
textile, sealed paper
PHOTOS BY CRAFT CENTER, ITAMY CITY, JAPAN

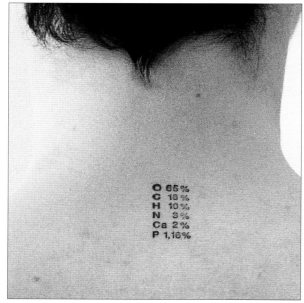

The connection to the body
shakes me. It reminds me of tattoos in
the Second World War. ■ *Ruudt Peters*

The simplicity of this design is outstanding, while at the same time, the engraving of the dates gives it something **poetic** and breaks the straightness of the perfectly round form. In jewelry, I prefer the use of nontraditional materials. For wedding rings, I like materials other than the obvious gold. This combination of materials is special: **warm wood and cool platinum**. I love the addition of a natural element in this sleek design. This ring reminds me of tree rings, which have to do with **growth and development**, which are also applicable to matrimony. ■ *Ingeborg Vandamme*

SORA MARUYAMA
From Mother Earth | 2005
LARGEST, 2.5 X 2.5 X 1.2 CM
Yakusugi (cedar), platinum
PHOTO BY ARTIST

A **clever nesting** of two basic geometric forms that also incorporates movement. ▪ *Jeff and Susan Wise*

ETSUKO SONOBE
Untitled | 2000
2.3 X 2.3 X 1.9 CM
20-karat gold
PHOTO BY OKINARI KUROKAWA

An **iconic** piece of jewelry. How do you make a ring set with a stone? Drill a hole in a piece of wood and mount the stone with four screws. **Simple and revolutionary.**
▪ *Mike Holmes*

MANUEL VILHENA
Untitled | 1999
3 X 2 X 1.5 CM
Oak, steel wood screws, uncut olivine; dyed
PHOTO BY ROB TURNER

In its simplicity, this ring is such a strong image. It's iconic, funny, original, back-to-basic, and "less is more." **It's perfect in its own way.** ▪ *Katja Prins*

I just love the way the stone is set in such a **rough, uncomplicated, and practical** way. A ring with a stone as plain as a ring with a stone can be. ▪ *Felieke van der Leest*

REBECCA STRZELEC
*Cross Section 9,
from Army-Green Orchids* | 2006
12 X 10.4 X 1.7 CM
FDM plastic, corsage pin;
rapid prototyped, CAD
PHOTOS BY DOUG YAPLE

This bracelet, while incorporating **space-age** titanium, has a thoroughly **organic** quality. The anodized discs put me in mind of wind-blown flower petals. ■ *Ann L. Lumsden*

HEATHER BAYLESS
Jingle Bangle | 2002
5 X 40 X 33 CM
Titanium, aluminum, sterling silver;
fabricated, riveted, anodized
PHOTO BY JEFF SABO

Julia Barello has taken a material, X-ray film, that most of us dismiss as either utilitarian or archaic, and reinvented a whole new vision that contains a conversation about the body in a thoroughly unexpected way. ▪ *Harriete Estel Berman*

JULIA M. BARELLO
Flowers of Rhetoric: Abcisio | 2007
61 CM IN DIAMETER
Recycled MRI film,
monofilament; laser cut
PHOTO BY MICHAEL O'NEILL

In this piece, I love the relationship between the material and the body that it adorns. Inside is brought outside, and the form facilitates the message, "flowering" from dense obscurity at the centers to recognition in the distal petals. The mystery of MRI imaging (most of us know what it is, but not specifically what it says) lends a layer of privacy to the brash exhibitionism of this piece, softening what could otherwise be an unsettling revelation of one human's condition. ▪ *Nisa Blackmon*

SARAH PERKINS
Leaf Neckpiece #1 | 1996
44 X 44 X 1.5 CM
Fine silver, sterling silver, enamel, stainless steel cable; formed, fabricated
PHOTOS BY TOM MILLS

I really had to **smile** when I saw these brilliant little brooches for the first time, ironically and with tongue-in-cheek posing as **imitations of nature** in which nature seems to be a masquerade of itself. ■ *Andrea Wagner*

SOFIA BJÖRKMAN
Wanna Be Precious | 2005
12 X 3 X 2 CM
Plastic flooring, carpet;
vacuum formed
PHOTO BY ARTIST

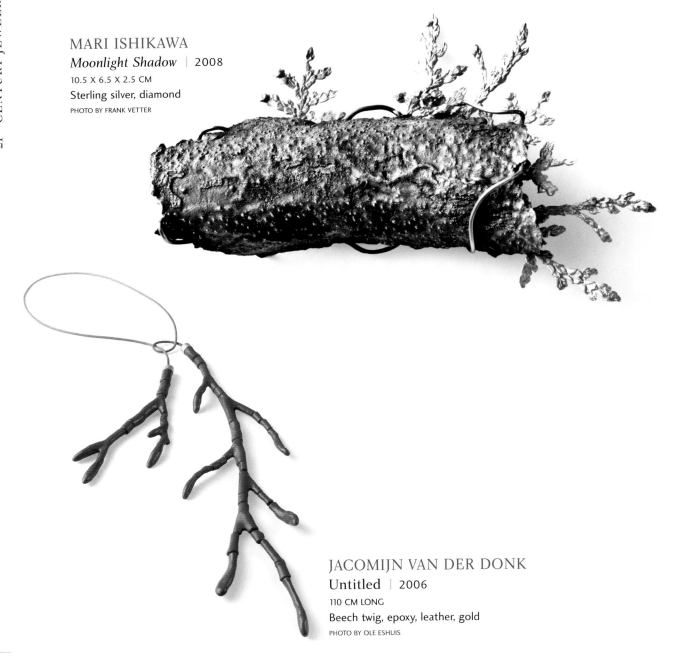

MARI ISHIKAWA
Moonlight Shadow | 2008
10.5 X 6.5 X 2.5 CM
Sterling silver, diamond
PHOTO BY FRANK VETTER

JACOMIJN VAN DER DONK
Untitled | 2006
110 CM LONG
Beech twig, epoxy, leather, gold
PHOTO BY OLE ESHUIS

I am quite absorbed with the notion of memory: what we choose to take away from our experiences, how we record them, and what is left behind after time has taken its toll. There is something **poignant** in Rebecca Hannon's methodical daily ritual of active remembering. By creating a **tangible visual record of her elusive memories**, she makes her journey more real and permanent. Although presented as mere shadows, the plant silhouettes drape and surround the body, **enveloping** the wearer in the past.

■ *Cappy Counard*

REBECCA HANNON
Camino de Santiago | 2004
10 X 600 X 0.3 CM
Rubber

PHOTO BY ARTIST
COURTESY OF MARZEE COLLECTION,
NIJMEGEN, THE NETHERLANDS

Brilliant and witty take on the necklace as throat ornamentation!

A beautiful piece, and a thoughtful and compelling image. ■ *Thomas Hill*

ANIKA SMULOVITZ
White Collar (4) | 2003
48 X 56 X 28 CM
Men's shirt collars; altered
PHOTO BY TOM MCINVAILLE
COLLECTION OF RACHELLE THIEWES

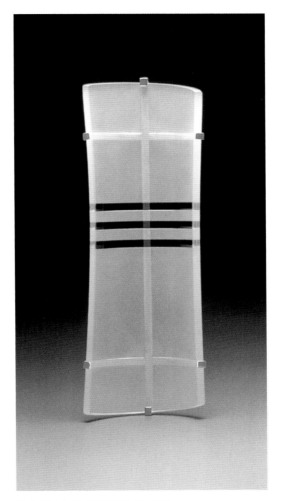

DONALD FRIEDLICH

Translucence Series Brooch | 2002

10.2 X 4.1 X 1.9 CM

Glass, 14-karat gold, 18-karat gold;
fabricated, carved, sandblasted

PHOTO BY JAMES BEARDS

Within the rigid confines of a gold frame is the **exquisite** and seemingly **fluid** movement of interlaced plastic tags. In this bold and elegant sculptural ring, the artist brilliantly **challenges the notion of value** by referencing price tags and combining expensive with inexpensive materials.

■ *Barbara Cohen*

CHRISTEL VAN DER LAAN
Priceless Gems! 2 | 2003
6.5 X 4 X 1.5 CM
18-karat gold, polypropylene
swing tags; fabricated
PHOTO BY ROBERT FRITH

I chose this exceptional piece because I am impressed with the level of **invention** in the design. **Found objects** have played a significant role in American jewelry. To me, there are two artists whose use of them rises above the rest, J. Fred Woell and Kiff Slemmons.

■ *Donald Friedlich*

KIFF SLEMMONS
Circumspect | 2003
31 X 28 X 1 CM
Silver, brass, mirror, lenses
PHOTO BY ROD SLEMMONS

This piece interests me for its **transforming qualities** as well as the amount of **diverse associations** I get when looking at it. ■ *Hanna Hedman*

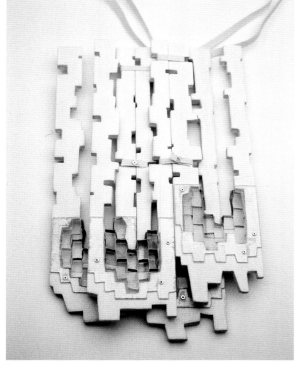

SETH PAPAC

Keep | 2007

20 X 6 X 6 CM

Poplar, gel stain, paint, architectural siding, 18-karat green gold, silver, elastic; hand fabricated, riveted

PHOTOS BY MARIA PHILLIPS

JOHAN VAN ASWEGEN
Fleur De Lys Earrings

Enamel, 18-karat gold; inlay, set

PHOTO BY ARTIST

The color, the shapes, the form, the **mixing of materials**—it is just breathtaking. ■ *Francis Willemstijn*

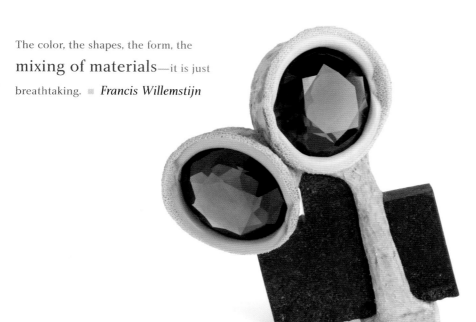

UTE EITZENHÖFER
Greetings from Idar-Oberstein 13 | 2007
7.5 X 6 X 2 CM
Smoky quartz, granite, plastic; welded
PHOTO BY JULIAN KIRSCHLER

LAURENCE OPPERMANN
Muraille | 2001
1.5 X 2.8 CM
Silver
PHOTO BY SYLVAIN PRETTO

A friend of mine told me about an art teacher she had at college who made her do drawings of lines. Using various brushes and drawing utensils, the students had to draw **page after page of lines**. Big brushes, small brushes, brushes with weights attached, brushes made from a single hair, sticks, stones, nails, feet…you name it. The exercise was intended for the students to make marks in as many ways as they could possibly think of and to analyze them afterwards. Bold, frail, confident, slow, fast, careless, concentrated, overindulgent, pretentious, shy…she told me these were some of the answers. Avoiding any decorative touches, it is the fine delicate drawing of the grid that reveals the pulse of the maker. **The beauty lies in what the ring is not**, and it is perfectly content with it. ■ *Klaus Burgel*

Even though it's a beautiful image, it's easy to imagine the power of the piece on the body—the range of **sounds** it will make, and the sense of **gravity** the motif brings, hanging from the neck, resting on the chest. It is carefully **orchestrated chaos** beautifully resolved.

■ *Castello Hansen*

JULIA TURNER
Untitled | 2005
11 X 8.5 X 3 CM
Ebony, steel, linen
PHOTO BY ARTIST

I'm drawn to the classic allure of the

facet reinterpreted

in gold and the marriage

of conceptualism and

craftsmanship in this ring.

■ *Mary Hallam Pearse*

KLAUS BURGEL
Untitled | 2000
4.4 X 3.2 X 2.3 CM
18-karat gold; hollow constructed
PHOTO BY MARK JOHNSTON

SABINE AMTSBERG
Untitled | 2001
2.7 X 3.6 X 1.4 CM
**Sterling silver, gold plate, bone;
forged, engraved**
PHOTO BY CHRISTOPH PAPSCH

CAROLINE GORE
Untitled | 2007
1.3 X 2.5 X 3 CM
Raw diamond, 18-karat gold
PHOTO BY ARTIST

The sentimental **memory** of searching for pyrite in the Virginia mountains is what quickly speaks to me in this piece. I have always admired Speckner's work; there is a way in which she **juxtaposes materials** that is simply spot on. ■ *Caroline Gore*

BETTINA SPECKNER
Brooch | 2003
2.5 X 4.5 X 2.5 CM
Pyrite, sapphire, gold
PHOTO BY ARTIST

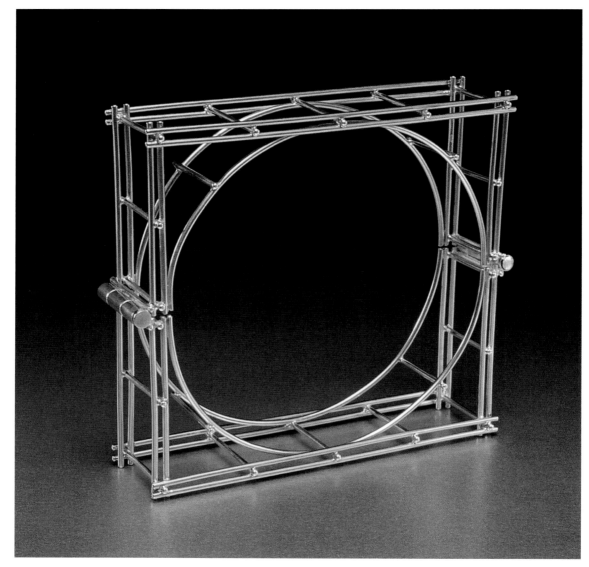

BEN NEUBAUER
Untitled | 2004
6 X 6.5 X 2 CM
Sterling silver, 18-karat gold; fabricated

I had the opportunity to try on a Philip Sajet ring once. It was not only very good looking, but also felt amazingly comfortable. I admire his **technical skills** in combination with his **beautiful designs**. In all his work, he makes good choices in size and proportion. The first impression of this ring is that precious stones are used, but the designer fools you in a **playful** way. He mainly uses "stones" of silver and pebbles with only a few little diamonds added.

Ingeborg Vandamme

PHILIP SAJET
Silverstone | 2002
1.6 X 3 X 2 CM
Silver stones, pebbles, diamonds
PHOTO BY BEATE KLOCKMANN

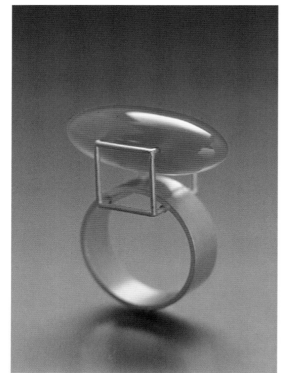

To set a stone requires an engineer's mind. For me, Etsuko Sonobe has gracefully combined **the skill and minimalism of an engineer with the aesthetic of an artist** while playing with all geometric forms. The warmth of the 20-karat yellow gold and the soft tones and shape of the carnelian contrast with the distinct geometrics of the fabricated setting. Brilliant! ■ *Janis Kerman*

ETSUKO SONOBE
Untitled | 2002
3.3 X 2.8 X 1.2 CM
20-karat gold, carnelian
PHOTO BY OKINARI KUROKAWA

ALBERTO ZORZI
The Town Ring | 2002
5 X 3 X 2.5 CM
18-karat gold
PHOTO BY MASSIMO SORMONTA

Always surprising, Michael understands the **optical properties** and **changing colors** of gemstones, combining them in his own way to let the chorus sing.

Thomas Herman

MICHAEL BOYD
Untitled | 2007
PENDANT, 4 X 3 X 1.5 CM
18-karat gold, 22-karat gold, sterling silver, Mexican opal, black jade, mookaite, imperial jadite pebble; fabricated
PHOTO BY STEVE BIGLEY

79

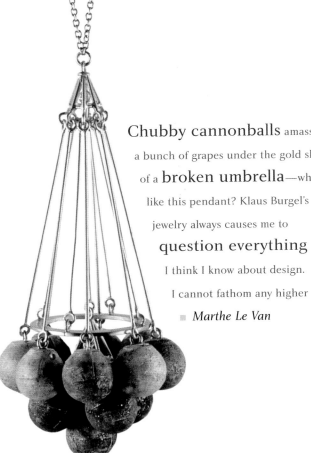

Chubby cannonballs amassed like a bunch of grapes under the gold skeleton of a **broken umbrella**—why do I like this pendant? Klaus Burgel's jewelry always causes me to **question everything** I think I know about design. I cannot fathom any higher praise.

■ *Marthe Le Van*

KLAUS BURGEL
Untitled | 1996
8.1 X 3.7 X 3.7 CM
18-karat gold, silver
PHOTO BY MARK JOHNSTON

This necklace is **delicate** yet so **strong** in appearance. I love the sawing she has used **like beautiful handwriting**. It takes me back in time and reminds me of old maps and graphics, which I love. ■ *Katja Prins*

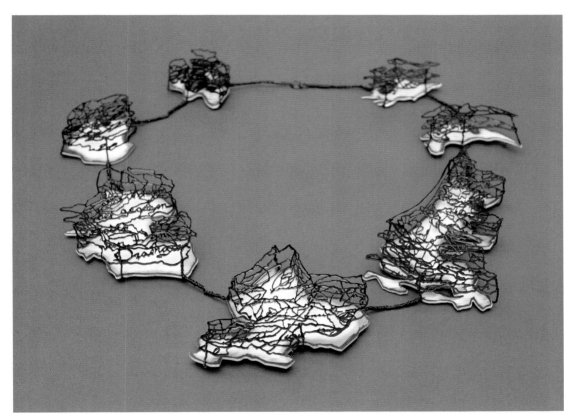

FRANCIS WILLEMSTIJN
Necklace for Willem van Oranje | 2007
40 CM IN LENGTH
Polystyrene, iron
PHOTO BY ARTIST

Sparkling golden glass is slumped—here convex, there concave—within the crevice of each of the earrings, apparently in conversation. There is pathos of **"human dilemma"** evoked in the contiguity of these little sculptures with the mood captured in the shadowed photograph. ■ *Beverley Price*

ANNAMARIA ZANELLA
Black | 2005
EACH, 3.5 X 2 X 1.5 CM
Silver, patina, glass, gold;
hand fabricated
PHOTO BY GIULIO RUSTICHELLI

ANNA HEINDL
Sunset | 2001
7 X 6 X 2 CM
18-karat gold, silver, citrines,
carnelian, sunstones; oxidized
PHOTO BY MANFRED WAKOLBINGER

The artist's **exotic** use of the deer fur speaks to my occasional use of wildebeest tail. **Radiating** lime-green spires, the grind-finished silver, and the asymmetry of wearing a single earring suggest visual "noise" beyond the form and the certain **engagement** of any viewer. ■ *Beverley Price*

TESSA E. RICKARD
Deer Talisman | 2006
10.2 X 10.2 X 0.3 CM
Sterling silver, dyed deer fur;
hand fabricated
PHOTO BY TIM CARPENTER

The title lets you start **thinking**.

The blood streams and gets solidified.

A **deep feeling** in a small piece.

■ *Ruudt Peters*

KADRI MÄLK
Medusa | 2004
9 X 6 X 2.4 CM
Oxidized silver, rubber
PHOTO BY TIIT RAMMUL

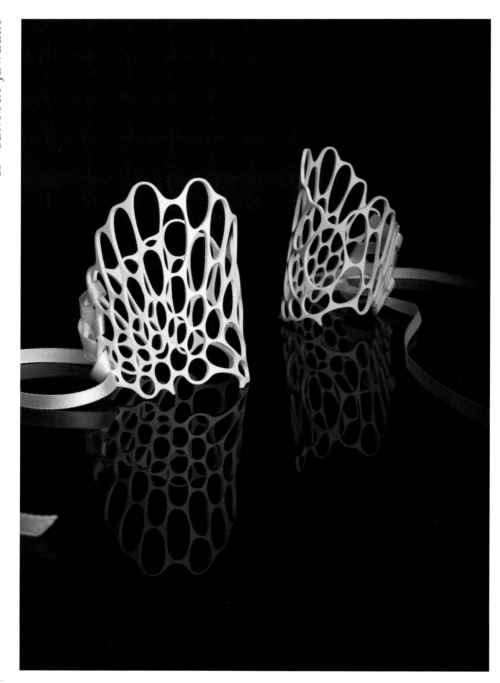

NERVOUS SYSTEM
JESSICA ROSENKRANTZ AND
JESSE LOUIS-ROSENBERG
Radiolaria Bracelet | 2007
0.2 X 7.6 X 15.7 CM
Silicone rubber, silk; water jet cut
PHOTO BY SARAH ST. CLAIR RENARD

Just start making a pattern, and it takes you on a holiday journey.

Nothing appears planned in the **randomness** of unstructured

repetition. Form and surface slowly **reveal** themselves.

Mary Hallam Pearse

SONIA MOREL
Untitled | 2004
8 X 9.5 X 3 CM
Silver, polyester thread
PHOTO BY ARTIST

The bright yellow color, the material, the manner in which multiples are worn, and the **startling scale** of these armlets made them favorites of mine since I first saw them. Kai Chan created armlets that are **simple and direct in technique, yet dynamic in form**. One special feature is that these armlets seem to change depending upon the **point of view** from which they are seen and the movement of the arm of the wearer. I continue to be fascinated by the ideas in these armlets and by their stunning beauty. ■ *Marjorie K. Schick*

KAI CHAN
Sunshine, White Sand Blue | 1984
7 X 34 X 30 CM AND 7 X 34 X 28 CM
Palm leaf, acrylic paint, thread;
hand fabricated
PHOTO BY ARTIST

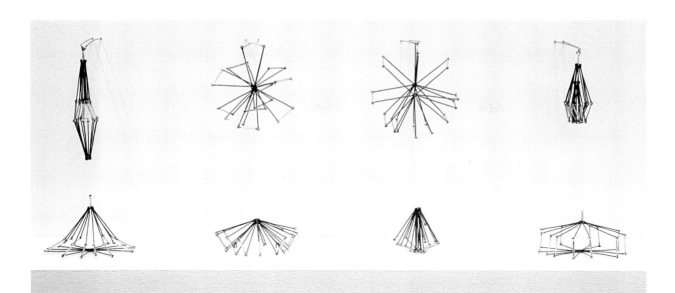

Delicate and kinetic, these earrings could be worn so many ways with beautiful symmetry and sculptural form. There are two artists that came to mind when I discovered Kristine Bolhuis' jewelry: Friedrich Becker and Alexander Calder. A master of kinetic jewelry, Becker also experimented with **changing composition of line** in his hinged brooches. Calder had a love affair with wire, from *Circus* to the hundreds of pieces he forged. Both artists would be good company for Bolhuis. Light, with a great sense of architecture and expression of pattern with movement, these earrings would be a joy to wear. ■ *Gina Pankowski*

KRISTINE BOLHUIS
An Earring Succumbs | 2003
INSTALLATION, 25 X 76 X 18 CM
Steel, 18-karat gold, wood;
hand fabricated with moveable joints
PHOTOS BY JOHN GUILLEMIN

Kristine's earrings are simultaneously **formal and mechanical, playful and organic**. She makes earrings interesting, and that is very difficult. ■ *Seth Papac*

I think this is so cool. In this piece, Geoff **transforms** from long dreadlocks to regular short hair. It is so fabulous to **document a life-changing moment** in this awesome piece of jewelry. ■ *Todd Reed*

GEOFFREY D. GILES

Self Portrait, Cultivated Perception | 2003

17.8 X 17.8 X 2.2 CM

Sterling silver, 18-karat yellow gold, human hair, acrylic, photographs; hand fabricated, hollow formed, brush finished, surface embellishment, riveted, oxidized

PHOTO BY TAYLOR DABNEY
COLLECTION OF MINT MUSEUM OF CRAFT + DESIGN, CHARLOTTE, NORTH CAROLINA

I love the **freedom** Marjorie gives us to **play** with the multiple elements and adorn ourselves at our own risk.

■ *Susan Kasson Sloan*

MARJORIE SCHICK
For Want of a Nail | 2001
CANVAS BROOCHES, 25.4 X 5.7 X 3.8 CM
STICK PINS, 16.5 X 2.5 CM
Canvas, wood, stainless steel wire;
stitched, stuffed, painted
PHOTOS BY GARY POLLMILLER

It's the use of metal in the context of photography that got my attention. We look at a **personal** snapshot right out of the family album. The setting is a residential street in a middle-class suburban neighborhood in the early '80s. We **witness** a proud moment. The brother is showing off his new motorcycle and gives his little sister a ride in front of the parents' house. We see the girl on the backseat and a boy, arms crossed, is looking on from a close distance. We cannot see the driver of the motorcycle though. He is a **suspiciously absent**, replaced with a featureless silhouette cut out from metal. The craftsmanship is daringly simple, but the **honesty of the moment** draws me in. There is pride in the girl's face as the two of them pose for the picture. The fact that the brother has been "mystified" heightens the affection and love she holds for him in a way more than the photo ever could. ▪ *Klaus Burgel*

CHARLOTTA NORRMAN
My Big Brother | 2001
20 X 30 X 5 CM
Photograph, medium-density fiberboard, silver
PHOTO BY ARTIST

KEITH A. LEWIS
Rapture | 1997
9 X 4.5 X 3 CM
Sterling silver, acrylic, paint
PHOTOS BY ARTIST

A young woman is looking at something in disbelief and horror. In reflex, she pulled her hands up to cover her mouth. Her hair is neatly tucked behind her ear. She is an observer, but **what does she see? We do not know.** Her wide-open eyes signal to us that the drama unfolds right now, right there. We could easily see it too, but we don't. Whatever it is she is seeing, she is not telling, and so everything around the wearer of this ring becomes **a moment of awe**, a constant moment of alert. ■ *Klaus Burgel*

MELANIE BILENKER
Observer | 2003
2.3 X 2 X 2.4 CM
18-karat gold, ivory piano-key laminate, epoxy resin, hair strands, watch crystal
PHOTO BY KEN YANOVIAK

MARIA VALDMA
Nora | 2003
6 X 4 CM
Wood, photocopy, silver; painted
PHOTO BY MIHKEL VALDMA

You can feel the **touch of the hammer** and the **heat of the torch** from every angle of this object. Monumental and intimate at the same time, *Under Construction* leaves you fascinated by the "evidence" of several metals and alloys and the **process of creation** itself.

■ *Talya Baharal*

FABRIZIO TRIDENTI
Under Construction | 2008

5.2 X 3.5 X 2.5 CM

Gold, silver, pure silver, copper, brass, various alloys; soldered, laminated, cut, welded, melted

PHOTO BY ARTIST

The combination and transition of color, material, texture, and shape create an off-kilter yet surprisingly and **beautifully balanced sculptural piece**. An apt title for this powerful brooch could easily be *The Tension of Balance*. ■ *Barbara Cohen*

HEE-SEUNG KOH
Collected Objects | 2003
6.7 X 8 X 1.5 CM
Sterling silver, paper, bamboo,
lapis lazuli, ironstone, ivory
PHOTO BY KWANG-CHOON PARK

A most beautiful and **heartfelt** piece. It is lovingly made with great skill and presents itself as a high-craft souvenir. A true **tour-de-force** of artistic strength. ■ *Lisa and Scott Cylinder*

CYNTHIA TOOPS
AND CHUCK DOMITROVICH

Mexico Trip | 2005

5 X 6.3 X 1 CM

Polymer clay, sterling silver

PHOTOS BY ROGER SCHREIBER
PRIVATE COLLECTION

This pair of earrings screams gravity. Amano has created a **physical and visual tension** between the bold, primary red, pregnant pod forms and the cascading botanical forms leading into them. There is even more tension from the ground to where it is anchored into the ear. Yet, the **flow and movement** of the earrings give them a comfortable lightness that would interact with the wearer. ■ *Michael Boyd*

SHIHOKO AMANO
Nazuna #1 | 2003
EACH, 7 X 2 X 2 CM
Sterling silver, boxwood, dye; fabricated
PHOTO BY KEN YANOVIAK

ROBERTA AND DAVID WILLIAMSON
I Long for Your Touch | 2001

9.5 X 6.4 X 1.3 CM

Sterling silver, quartz crystal, shell, abalone, brass,
antique lithograph; fabricated, formed, soldered

PHOTO BY JAMES BEARDS

White noise, our mind's mechanism to protect us from auditory overstimulation. This necklace, with its **collection of memories** in the form of objects, symbols, and charms, could be a physical representation in a broader sense—perhaps for meditating on one's experience as you look at and feel the symbols of memory. The noise the piece makes is **soothing** to the wearer, and the weight of the piece creates a sense of **comfort**, a hug from your past. ■ *Gina Pankowski*

Beautiful use of white material.

■ *Sigurd Bronger*

Robin Ayres assembles the tiny bits and pieces that accumulate in our junk drawers to create an intriguing, **intimate** necklace. She sorts through generations of minutia, such as trinkets of **sentimental** reminiscences left over from past-life moments. *White Noise* is an old, ghost-like photo holding memories without meaning.

■ *Harriete Estel Berman*

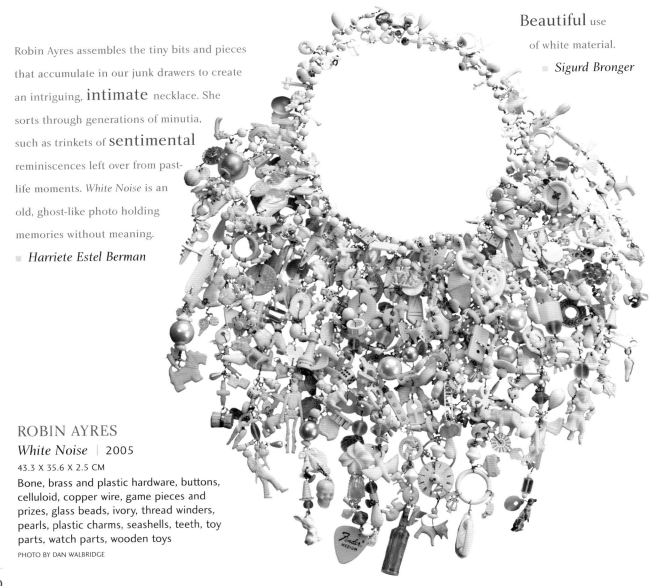

ROBIN AYRES

White Noise | 2005

43.3 X 35.6 X 2.5 CM

Bone, brass and plastic hardware, buttons, celluloid, copper wire, game pieces and prizes, glass beads, ivory, thread winders, pearls, plastic charms, seashells, teeth, toy parts, watch parts, wooden toys

PHOTO BY DAN WALBRIDGE

This bracelet launches a multi-faceted dialog about value: the value of **craftsmanship**, the value of **materials**, the creation of an **identity** as a maker, and the value of jewelry. It conveys intelligence in the content **message** and the thoughtful assembly of symbolic slivers of money.

Harriete Estel Berman

KATHY BUSZKIEWICZ
Lining: The United States of America | 2004
7.4 X 11.4 X 11.4 CM
Sterling silver, U.S. currency, wood;
hand fabricated, engraved, lathe turned
PHOTOS BY ARTIST

This reminds me
of a recurring
dream that is
now **forgotten**.
■ *Namu Cho*

TOM MUIR
Dream Suite | 2007
17.3 X 13 X 3.5 CM
Fabricated, electroformed, cast, machined
PHOTO BY TIM THAYER

KEN THIBADO
Light Weight Earrings | 2006
EACH, 5.7 X 1.5 X 1.4 CM
14-karat gold, sapphires, antique pin backs, light bulbs;
hand fabricated, bezel set, tube set
PHOTO BY ROBERT DIAMANTE

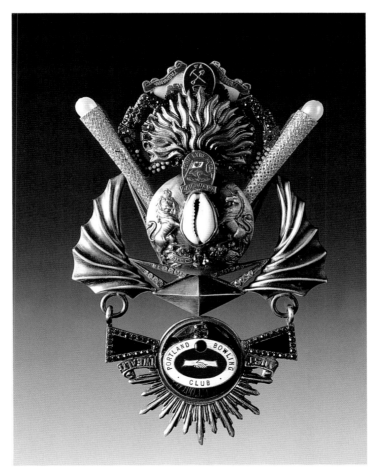

PIERRE CAVALAN

Dieu Est Mon Droit | 1994

18.5 X 12 X 3.5 CM

Found objects; assembled

PHOTO BY JULIAN WOLKENSTEIN

This piece is **engaging and playful**. Materials such as river rocks, beach glass, and, in this case, shark teeth, can be very cliché. Milheiro has **raised the bar** and avoided cliché by using these elements conceptually, creating an animated narrative.

■ *Michael Boyd*

TERESA MILHEIRO
Ripper | 2002
1 X 5 X 8 CM
Silver, shark teeth;
hand fabricated, oxidized
PHOTO BY LUIS PAIS

The crude **roughness** of the materials is in contrast to the **sophistication** of the designs. Each setting in the trio complements the piece of fossil and all together makes a **balanced** grouping. ■ *Barbara Cohen*

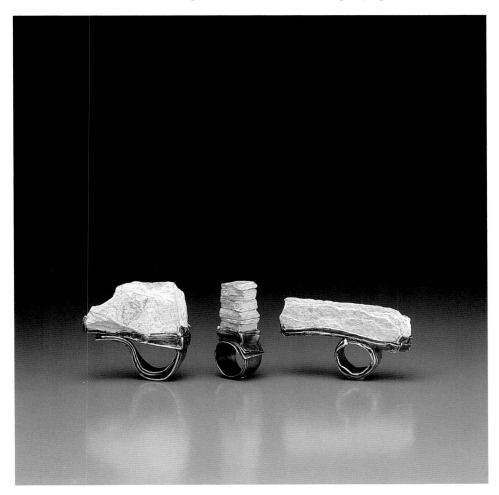

SEUNG JIN LEE

Impression | 2002

5 X 5.2 X 1.2 CM (LEFT); 4 X 2.3 X 1.8 CM (CENTER);
3.6 X 6.9 X 1 CM (RIGHT)

Silver, fish fossil; wax cast

PHOTO BY MYUNG-WOOK HUH (STUDIO MUNCH)

Things can **burst apart,** and their pieces will be carried all over the world. But sometimes fragments **find their way back** to each other in some mysterious manner. And then, only pink scars tell of former injuries and fractures.

■ *Beate Eismann*

JOSÉE DESJARDINS
Lost at Sea II | 2004
4.8 X 15.9 X 14 CM
Found wood, cotton thread; hand fabricated
PHOTO BY ANTHONY MCLEAN

ANDREA WAGNER
Instrumentrics #12 | 1998
4.5 X 7 X 4.5 CM
Sterling silver, epoxy resin, pigment;
rolled, sawed, bent, soldered, multi-cast,
sand finished, polished
PHOTO BY ILSE SCHRAMA

Adorning one's body with jewelry is an expressive act that is performed on countless levels. Wearing mourning jewelry is one of the most **ritualistic and talismanic** customs. The eventual disintegration of the silk and the survival of the silver is a most **poignant** conclusion. ■ *Marthe Le Van*

MIRIAM VERBEEK
Rouwring (Mourning Ring) | 1993
10 X 15 X 2.5 CM
Silver, silk, net; crocheted
PHOTO BY HENNIE VAN BEEK

GIOVANNA IMPERIA
Flexibility—Shapeable Bracelet | 2004
6.4 X 17.8 CM
Coated copper wire, sterling silver;
hand woven, hand fabricated
PHOTO BY JACK B. ZILKER

Knitting with chain—what a great use of a material in a way it was not designed to be used. The drape of chain mail with a sparkle…a beautiful, flexible fabric of silver. ■ *Mary Lee Hu*

FLORA BOOK
Wrap for an Octopus | 2004
45 X 100 CM
Sterling silver; knitted, woven
PHOTO BY ROGER SCHREIBER

From a series, this pendant is particularly interesting for being **ambiguous**. In it, there is a sense of **nihilism** at the same time as an extravasation of a **secret belief**. ■ *Leonor Hipólito*

EVERT NÝLAND
Pendant | 1997
15 X 13 X 1.5 CM
Iron, mole fur, glass, silver, velvet cord; cast
PHOTO BY KAI SCHIEFER
PRIVATE COLLECTION

INGEBORG VANDAMME
Poetry-Container | 1995
PENDANT, 2.5 X 10.5 CM
Copper, paper; etched
PHOTO BY RON ZIJLSTRA
PRIVATE COLLECTION

I am attracted to the concept of **wearing your thoughts** as an extension of the
body, and I am curious about the subject of all the words. ■ *Hanna Hedman*

ELIZABETH RYAN
Thoughts | 2005
LARGEST, 2 X 16 X 0.1 CM
Aluminum wire, thread;
formed, powder coated
PHOTOS BY ADAM KRAUTH

A piece to **think** about.
■ *Suzanne Esser*

At first, this necklace called my attention, and then it made
me think how it could have been made differently. It is about
thoughts, and it **triggers** thoughts. ■ *Leonor Hipólito*

KATH INGLIS
Skin-Deep Bangles | 2001
EACH, 3.3 X 7 X 7 CM
PVC, sterling silver; fabricated,
hand colored, hand carved, hand stitched
PHOTO BY MICHAEL HAINES

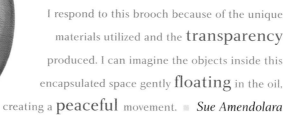

MARZIA ROSSI
Ice | 2002
5 X 4.5 X 0.9 CM
Thermoplastic, silver, glass, oil
PHOTO BY FEDERICO CAVICCHIOLI

I respond to this brooch because of the unique materials utilized and the **transparency** produced. I can imagine the objects inside this encapsulated space gently **floating** in the oil, creating a **peaceful** movement. ■ *Sue Amendolara*

Sprung from the working method that Svenja John has been applying for many years, this brooch introduces a **saucy nuance** into the artist's work. The fresh green color seems to want to break through geometry's logics, and soon it will **grow and run wild**. ■ *Beate Eismann*

Ingeniously engineered and constructed, creating a beautiful controlled bundle of transparent fragile elements that remind us of **organic cells**.
■ *Charon Kransen*

Colorful, playful, light, wearable, touchable, and **highly original**.
■ *Kathryn Wardill*

THOMAS MANN
float series—animated heart | 2004
8.9 X 6.4 CM
Silver, acrylic, brass, bronze
PHOTO BY ANGELE SEILEY

SVENJA JOHN
Breath Brooch | 2001
4 X 9 CM IN DIAMETER
Polycarbonate; surface treated, constructed, colored
PHOTO BY SILKE MAYER

The works from this collection are simply beautiful because of their originality, strong compositions, and odd shapes and materials. **They make me wonder**, which to me is one of the best emotions in life. ■ *Katja Prins*

Fragile and strong. Man- and woman-like. Soft foam with hard and breakable porcelain. **These rings look like they have always been here.** ■ *Francis Willemstijn*

JANTJE FLEISCHHUT
Pedal | 2002
5.5 X 3.5 X 4 CM
Fiberglass, silver; constructed
PHOTO BY EDDO HARTMANN

IRIS EICHENBERG
Untitled | 1998
4 X 4.5 X 1.5 CM
Silver, porcelain, medical foam; cast
PHOTO BY RON ZIJLSTIA

Masterfully engineered, this cuff has so many **intricate** layers you can't help but be drawn in to explore it further. It has an **ethereal glow** that radiates out with its graceful soft spokes.

emiko oye

ANASTASIA AZURE
Egg Hunt | 2007

20 X 20 X 20 CM

Nylon monofilament, color pigment, wire; dimensional weave, inlaid

MAIN PHOTO BY HAP SAKWA
DETAIL PHOTO BY TOM MCINVAILLE

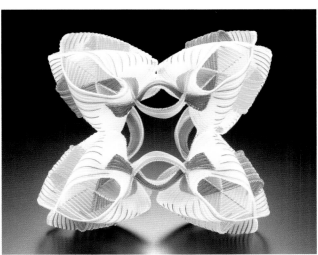

My interest in this necklace starts with the **subtle** and safe pastel palette. McCreary has then contrasted this with a very pleasing awkwardness created by the use of **out-of-balance** opposing elements in both shape and space.

■ *Michael Boyd*

KAREN MCCREARY
Geode Pendant | 1999
12 X 2.5 X 1.5 CM
Acrylic, 22-karat gold leaf,
sterling silver; carved,
hand fabricated
PHOTO BY ARTIST

KENNETH C. MACBAIN
Necklace | 2008
54 X 21 X 1 CM
Acrylic, sterling silver;
fabricated, riveted
PHOTO BY ARTIST

This untitled piece has a wide look around the neck but flows nicely and appears easy to wear. I enjoy the artist's use of **lightly colored transparency** and subtle use of **linear pattern** flowing in each section. ■ *Linda MacNeil*

BETTY HEALD
Untitled | 1998

18 X 23 X 1 CM

Acrylic, sterling silver, elastic cord;
heat formed, fabricated, chemically dyed

PHOTO BY HOLMES/BLAKESLEE-LANE

The ethereal, almost halo-like creation is an example of stunning craftsmanship, **avant-garde creativity**, and vision. It delivers a conceptual message through unexpected materials and with a sense of humor. ▪ *Nina Basharova*

I am struck by the way that Christel van der Laan transforms a mundane object into something intriguing and gem-like. Presented en masse, the plastic swing tags are disconnected from their original purpose and serve instead to create a subtle play of **light, density, and texture**. It is such a simple solution that yields alluring and surprisingly **tactile** results. Although I have only seen images of this piece, I can imagine how the interior surface would feel against my wrist and the sound it would make as it moved. ▪ *Cappy Counard*

CHRISTEL VAN DER LAAN
Priceless Bangle | 2004
24 X 24 X 4 CM
18-karat gold plate, sterling silver, polypropylene swing tags; fabricated
PHOTOS BY ROBERT FRITH

Wow! Talk about **sparkling** blue eyes! ● *Ann L. Lumsden*

ANGELA EBERHARDT
The Ultimate Accessory | 2008
1.3 X 3.2 X 2.2 CM
Medical-grade acrylic,
black diamonds, chocolate diamonds,
blue sapphires, cubic zirconia
PHOTOS BY ARTIST

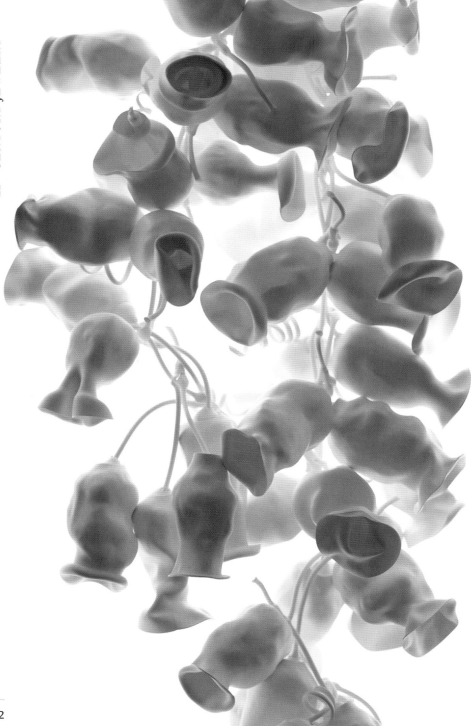

Frozen in time, these **pure** petals are the result of an **ingenious** but **logical** use of a utilitarian product's intended properties, but they are then launched into a new **poetic** existence that is incredibly beautiful.

■ *Andrea Wagner*

SUSANNE KLEMM
Boa (Necklace) | 2007
35 X 4 X 4 CM
Polyolefin; thermoformed
PHOTO BY HAROLD STRAK

This piece **evokes the essence of "brooch"** in its purity of color and form, edited down to such a **simple statement of beauty.** I even love how the tips of the pin stems peak out from the back. If a brooch can be a poem, this is surely it.

Deborah Lozier

SEUNG HYE CHOI
Spring Snow | 2002
5.3 X 5.3 X 7 CM
Sterling silver, enamel
PHOTO BY STUDIO MUNCH

STEVEN FORD AND DAVID FORLANO

Bubble Necklace | 2004

7 X 50 X 5 CM

Polymer clay, sterling silver; cast, inlaid

PHOTO BY ROBERT DIAMANTE

I enjoy the artist's ability to **transform** a relatively mundane **material** into something supple, tactile, and beautiful.

■ *Jessica Calderwood*

A most unusual material—balloons, creates a naturalistic, tactile feel. They have a sense of **romance, tenderness,** and the **fragility** of flowers.

■ *Nina Basharova*

MEGAN AUMAN
Poppies! | 2003
17 X 17 X 10 CM
Balloons, copper; hand fabricated, sewn
PHOTO BY NATHAN DUBE

500 Plastic Jewelry Designs is a book
I always refer back to with great pleasure.
The joyful works contained within
**allude to all that jewelry
might become in the
future**. I love Liaung Chung Yen's use
of repurposed materials in her poetic
Changeability ring. ■ *Rebecca Hannon*

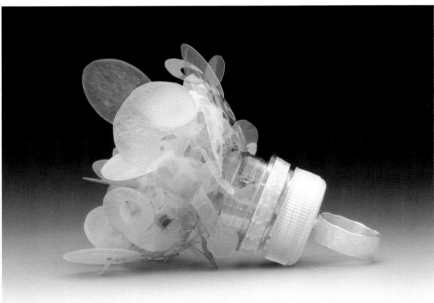

LIAUNG CHUNG YEN
Changeability #1 (Pendant/Ring) | 2007
8 X 8 X 8 CM
Plastic bottle and cap, plastic sheet,
sterling silver; cut, fabricated
PHOTOS BY ARTIST

ANN L. LUMSDEN
Bellybutton Ornament | 2007

6.1 CM IN DIAMETER

18-karat white gold, 18-karat yellow gold,
silk flowers, diamond; cast, constructed

PHOTOS BY ARTIST

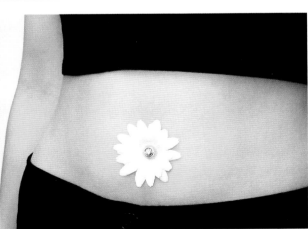

Although I don't like jewelry made of gold so much, this one is an exception. **The color of the gold is beautiful.** It looks like a textile. The rough stones are beautiful in the gold setting.

■ *Miriam Verbeek*

RIAN DE JONG
From the Series NY-NY | 2008
4.5 X 3 X 1 CM
Cordierite, peridot, copper, gold; electroformed
PHOTO BY ARTIST

Playful design, **organic** and **lustrous.**

An **inventive** way of using enamels.

■ *Kathryn Wardill*

JESSICA MORRISON
Yellow; Blue and Yellow | 2004
EACH, 3.5 X 10 X 9.5 CM
Fine silver, 24-karat gold,
sterling silver, enamel; fused
PHOTO BY TERENCE BOGUE

This ring is a **point of dialogue** between handicraft and art. Starting with traditional materials and traditional ring structure, **the rigid laws of the goldsmith's craft are totally upset** in a revolution based on a big dose of irony and personality. The stone is no longer the main component of the ring. Its value and beauty are cancelled by the artist's idea and work. A new value appears from this, which is much more interesting to me. ■ *Fabrizio Tridenti*

Clearly Karl was not looking for perfection in the sense of being neat, clean, straight, or round. Humor, courage, conviction, confidence are the virtues that make this ring. A very **sensual but clever** little ring that leaves no page of jewelry's history unturned, no can of worms unopened. ■ *Klaus Burgel*

KARL FRITSCH
Ruby Ring I | 2002
3 X 2 X 1 CM
Gold, ruby; cast
PHOTO BY ARTIST

Placed among wildly distinctive rings, Karl's looks inconspicuous. It is sensitively formed, **kneaded** with the ruby set **aslant**. It gives me an impression of **tenderness,** as if it were done in the earliest of times.
■ *Pavel Herynek*

KARL FRITSCH
Untitled | 2006
2.8 X 2.5 X 1.5 CM
Gold, diamonds, rubies, emeralds; cast
PHOTO BY ARTIST

Unabashedly beautiful, *Lumen #9* masterfully **champions the richness and spirit of ornament** without appearing "precious" or "pretty." Delicate painting, microscopic patterns, and rich color and surface combine in a **slightly eccentric** format. This instills a sense of Bennett being playfully "at ease" with his **technical virtuosity** while probing the transient nature of life. ■ *Wendy McAllister*

Jamie produces beautiful, **painterly** enamel surfaces complemented by 18-karat gold. Though technically **impeccable**, each of his pieces presents with a feeling of **spontaneity**, which I love—the sign of a true artist.

■ *Susan Kasson Sloan*

JAMIE BENNETT
Lumen #9 | 2002
4.7 X 5 X 0.6 CM
Enamel, 18-karat gold
PHOTO BY KEVIN SPRAGUE

I would wear this. The **attitude of craftsmanship** thrills me. I love and respect the challenge of the **mechanics** involved in such a design. The open linear quality of the construction with transparent **moving jewels** appears very lightweight. I can guess they have a nice **sound** to them while being worn. ■ *Linda MacNeil*

YAEL SONIA
Perpetual Motion: Spinning Wheel | 2000
8.3 CM IN DIAMETER
18-karat yellow gold, blue topaz, diamonds;
hand constructed
PHOTO BY ALMIR PASTORE

The color play is **genius**.
The Mexican fire opal is a fantastic
rare specimen showcasing
lots of color with opaque and
translucent qualities. The blue
and cognac diamonds encircling
the center stone bring out many
of the **uncommon** color flashes
and complement the natural orange tones.

Cindy Edelstein

VICENTE AGOR
Vesuvius Ring | 2007
3.8 X 2.5 X 1.6 CM
18-karat gold, blue diamonds, cognac diamonds,
Mexican fire opal; lost wax cast, hand carved
PHOTO BY MIKE PFEFFER

MARK SCHNEIDER
Tourmaline Switchback Earrings | 2007
EACH, 3.5 X 1.1 X 7 CM
18-karat white gold, white diamonds,
yellow diamonds, green tourmalines
PHOTO BY JOHN PARRISH

The simple profile of these two rings is **elegance personified**. Makes me wish I had made them first. ■ *Nanz Aalund*

YESIM YUKSEK
Gothic Bride + Deco Bride | 2006
TALLEST, 3.3 X 2.3 X 0.8 CM
Sterling silver, white cubic zirconia,
18-karat yellow gold; cast, hand fabricated,
soldered, constructed, bezel set
PHOTOS BY ADIL GUMUSOGLU

My personal taste in jewelry runs the gamut from very minimal and contemporary to Art Deco and early 1900s design. I think Glik's *Floating Chandelier Earrings* speak to this gut instinct. I love the "non-color" aspect and the **craftsmanship** that these **gorgeous specimens** display. I wish I could own them! ■ *Janis Kerman*

MORITZ GLIK
Floating Chandelier Earrings | 2008
EACH, 7.5 X 4 X 0.5 CM
Diamonds, clear quartz crystal, 18-karat white gold
PHOTO BY PAULO FILGUEIRAS

GURHAN
Eternity Rose-Cut Diamond Ring | 2006
2.5 X 2.5 X 0.6 CM
Platinum, white and champagne rose-cut diamonds;
hand fabricated
PHOTO BY RALPH GABRINER

The overall simplicity with the **bang** of the gold and the pink. Gorgeous heavily slanted bezel!

■ *Joanna Gollberg*

MARK NUELL
Untitled | 2008
4 X 3 X 2 CM
18-karat gold, 22-karat gold,
pink tourmaline; forged, set
PHOTO BY FXP PHOTOGRAPHY

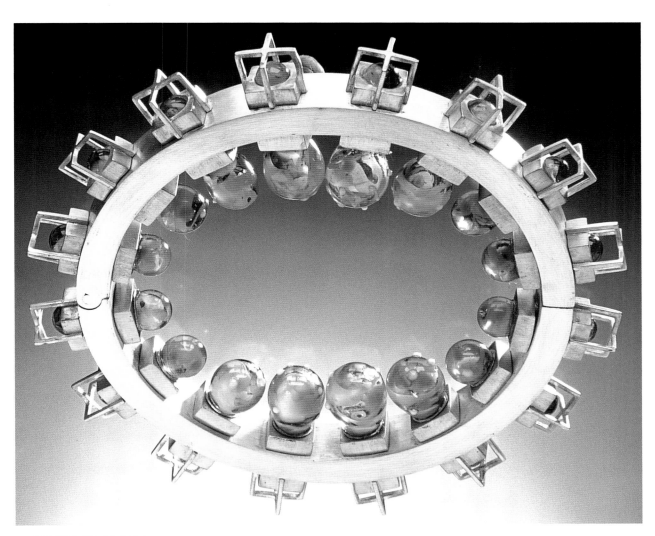

LAUREN KALMAN
Diffusion | 2002
8 X 8 X 1 CM
Sterling silver, 14-karat gold,
glass; hollow constructed,
cast, lampworked, hinged
PHOTO BY DEAN POWELL

BABETTE VON DOHNANYI
Untitled | 2007
EACH, 3 X 2.5 X 2 CM
Sterling silver, amethyst,
rose crystal; cut, cast
PHOTO BY FEDERICO CAVICCHIOLI

LULU SMITH
Petal Necklace | 2005
2.5 X 50 X 0.5 CM
Sterling silver, resin, pigment;
cast, hand fabricated, inlaid
PHOTO BY DOUG YAPLE

I admire this ring and wish it was mine every time I see it. I adore the **colors**, the **shapes**, and the way all those stones are stacked up together. I like its **spontaneity** and sense of **humor**. It makes me smile.

■ *Daphne Krinos*

KARL FRITSCH
Die Tränen von Pandora | 2004
8 X 6 X 5 CM
Silver, various stones; oxidized
PHOTO BY ARTIST

Such a beauty.
  Ralph Bakker

STEPHANIE JENDIS
Montblanc | 2005
6 X 3.5 X 2.5 CM
Ebony, ivory, amethyst, 18-karat gold
PHOTO BY ARTIST

This piece of fiberglass has
a fabulous brightness and
lightness. Through
a **perfect**
combination
of **materials**,
it is made into a
wonderful brooch.
  Birgit Laken

This found piece of plastic becomes **powerful**
once the stones are added. You can give the piece
your own story. *Ruudt Peters*

STEPHANIE JENDIS
Mallorca | 2003
7.5 X 16 X 1 CM
Synthetic resin, fiberglass,
synthetic stones, silver
PHOTO BY RON ZIJLSTRA

I really want to touch this piece! It has an **edgy tactility** that makes me want to pet it. Davies has used a comfortable pallet of **harmonious colors** complemented with a touch of green that calmly keeps this piece awake and alive. ■ *Michael Boyd*

JENNACA LEIGH DAVIES
Untitled | 2006
5 X 4 X 4 CM
Copper, sterling silver, enamel
PHOTOS BY STEFFEN KNUDSEN ALLEN

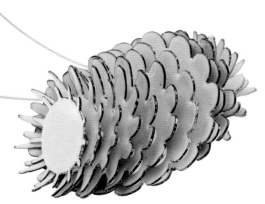

An interesting engineering mind. **Building form from repeated shapes.** Light and flexible with a soft noise as the elements slide against each other. ■ *Mary Lee Hu*

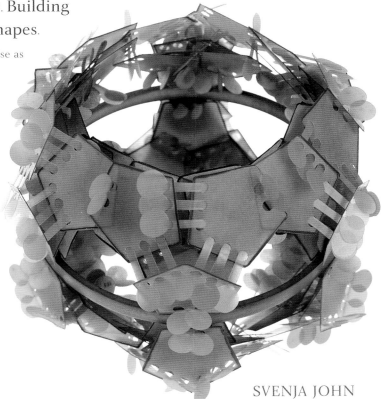

SVENJA JOHN
Vize | 2002
9 X 20 CM IN DIAMETER
Polycarbonate; hand fabricated,
hand colored
PHOTO BY SILKE MAYER

An **interpretation** of **nature** at its best.

◼ *Michael Good*

BARBARA HEINRICH
Untitled | 1990
EACH, 6.2 X 2.5 X 1 CM
18-karat yellow gold, diamonds, pearls;
chased, hand fabricated, bezel set
PHOTO BY TIM CALLAHAN

GARRY VANNAUSDLE

Wheat Design Wedding Bands | 2006

EACH, 0.7 X 0.7 CM

14-karat yellow gold, diamond;
hard wax carved, lost wax cast, recarved, set

PHOTO BY ARTIST

NORIKO SUGAWARA

Morning Dew | 2004

EACH, 3 X 3 X 1 CM

18-karat gold, moonstones, diamonds; hand fabricated

PHOTO BY RALPH GABRINER

ALEX SEPKUS

Alex Sepkus Orchard Ring | 2008

LARGE STONE, 1.1 CM IN DIAMETER

18-karat rose gold, faceted round sapphires, diamonds

PHOTO BY ARUNAS KULIKAUSKAS

Lilly brings a true **reverence for nature** forward, showing us the beauty contained in each mineral.

■ *Thomas Herman*

The 22-karat gold glowing through the translucence of this beautiful agate completes the almost **spiritual illusion** of a lone tree emerging from the fog. The mysterious chop on the metalwork accentuates its totem-like feeling. It is a **powerfully serene** piece. ■ *George Sawyer*

LILLY FITZGERALD
Pin | 2000
7.6 X 1.9 CM
22-karat gold, agate;
hand fabricated
PHOTO BY ARTIST

MICHAEL GOOD
Untitled | 2000
EACH, 3.2 CM IN DIAMETER
18-karat gold; hand formed, anticlastic
raising, polished, sandblasted
PHOTO BY PAM MARRACINI

JAMES E. BINNION
Mokume Wedding Ring | 2004
0.9 X 0.2 CM
14-karat palladium white gold,
sterling silver, 18-karat yellow gold;
mokume gane
PHOTO BY HAP SAKWA

Hands down, probably the most **captivating, unforgettable** image of five simple rings—each and every one is the finest example of a new take on ancient technique. The visual impact of fluid and capricious patterns is **masterfully doubled in perfect symmetry**, underlined with a fine golden line. ▪ *Nina Basharova*

GEORGE SAWYER

Primitive Symmetry | 2000

EACH, 2.5 X 0.6 X 2.5 CM

14-karat gray gold, sterling silver, 22-karat yellow gold; pattern matched edge grain mokume gane, fabricated

PHOTO BY PETER LEE

While the technical execution of Ryan's work is **impeccable,** it's the pure beauty she creates through the **elegant forms** she constructs that constantly catches my eye and holds my attention.

■ *Sim Luttin*

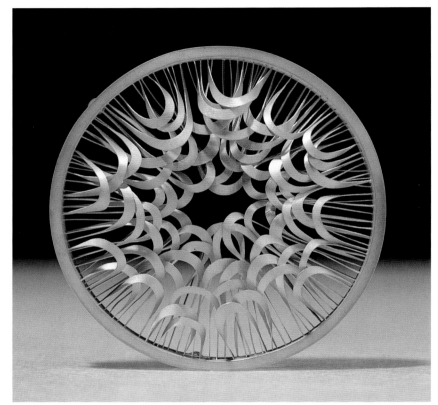

JACQUELINE RYAN
Brooch | 2000
6 CM IN DIAMETER
18-karat gold; fabricated
PHOTO BY GIOVANNI CORVAJA

The **thoughtfulness** of these rings really speaks to me. I like how the man's ring is designed from a square and has a very hard edge while the woman's ring is designed from a circle and has a very **sensual** burnished edge. And yet with the two different shapes, you have these wonderful pod forms that show the **unity** between the rings and people. ■ *Geoffrey D. Giles*

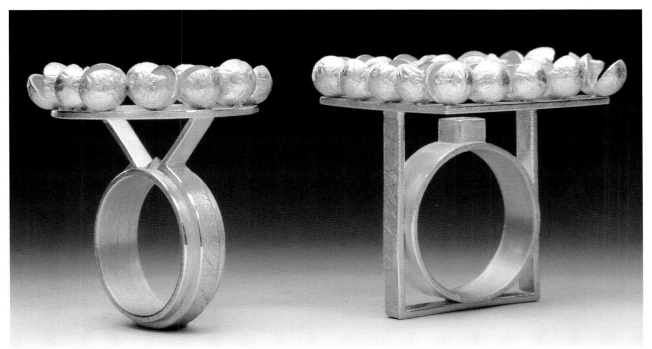

LIAUNG CHUNG YEN

Flourishing #6 & #7 | 2006

AVERAGE, 3.5 X 2.5 X 2.5 CM

18-karat gold, diamonds,
brown diamonds; fabricated

PHOTOS BY ARTIST

Amazing. Reminiscent of Indian Kundan stone setting, but in a more **formal, perfect** way. The carving makes this ring a true treasure. ■ *Joanna Gollberg*

EMRE DILAVER
Untitled | 2007
3.8 X 3 X 3.5 CM
24-karat gold, sterling silver,
lemon topaz, diamonds;
set, carved
PHOTOS BY LEVENT YÜCEL

Lori's roots in tradition shine through her work, making us stop to **contemplate the depth**. *Thomas Herman*

LORI TALCOTT
Mardöll II | 2002
12 X 9.5 X 2.5 CM
Silver, 18-karat gold; fabricated
PHOTO BY DOUGLAS YAPLE

Beautiful work and presentation on the hand.
After seeing this image for several years, I can't stop thinking about it. *Tom Muir*

MARIANNE ANDERSON
Fragments of Ornament Necklace | 2007
15 X 20 CM
Silver, 18-karat gold, garnets,
pearls; oxidized
PHOTO BY ARTIST

MARY PRESTON

Cameo Chimera | 2002

4.4 X 2.5 X 0.6 CM

18-karat gold, silver, steel, pearls;
cut, fabricated, repoussé

PHOTO BY RALPH GABRINER

ANYA KIVARKIS

Brooch | 2003

7 X 5.5 X 3.5 CM

Copper, enamel, sterling silver;
die formed, fabricated

PHOTO BY ARTIST

RALPH BAKKER
Untitled | 2008
20 CM IN DIAMETER
Gold, tantalum, lemon quartz
PHOTO BY ARTIST

I like this work so much. It is **bold** in its frame, but so **fragile** and **chaotic** inside. Inside is fighting to get out in a **tangled** reality. Truly beautiful and amazing.

■ *Todd Reed*

GIOVANNI CORVAJA
Brooch | 1998
7 X 7 X 1.2 CM
24-karat gold, platinum; granulated

PHOTOS BY ARTIST

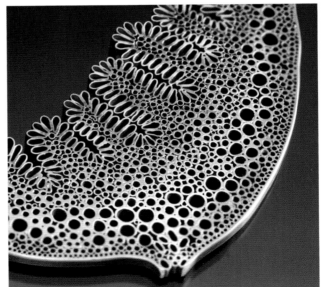

VINA RUST

Eastern Cottonwood Defense | 2008

10.1 X 7.6 X 0.3 CM

Sterling silver, 14-karat gold, liver-of-sulfur
patina; hand fabricated, oxidized

PHOTOS BY DOUG YAPLE

SAYUMI YOKOUCHI
Kanzashi Earring 3 | 2003
EACH, 5.7 X 1 CM
18-karat yellow gold
PHOTO BY RALPH GABRINER

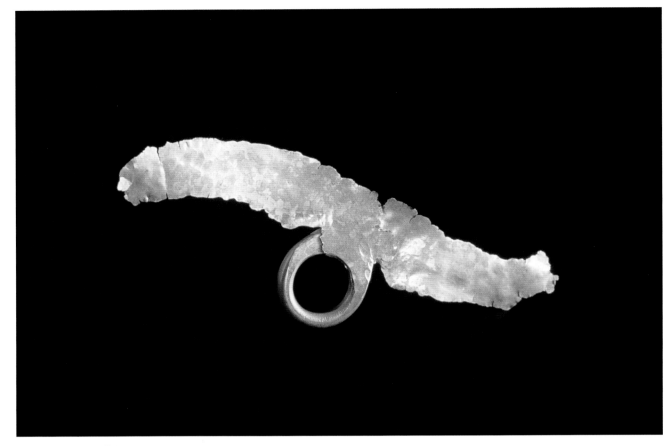

SHARI PIERCE
Ring | 2000
5 X 17.8 CM
Sterling silver; forged
PHOTO BY ARTIST

I chose this ring for its **material tension**
and **timelessness**. When was it made?
Was it made by mistake? ■ *Hanna Hedman*

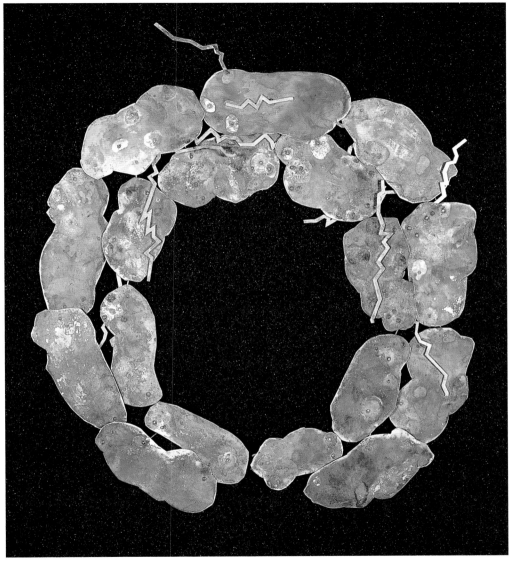

PHILIP SAJET
Thunder & Lightning | 1994

20 X 30 CM

Silver, gold

PHOTO BY ARTIST
COLLECTION OF THE STEDELYK MUSEUM,
AMSTERDAM, THE NETHERLANDS

This necklace is very dear to me. It thoroughly fascinated me during my training as a young goldsmith. I remember the catalog where I saw it for the first time, *Elf Colliers*. It is a successful example of **combining narrative elements in the construction of a jewel**, while avoiding an ordinary or common result.

■ *Stefano Marchetti*

Exactly what its title says. Let's get our umbrellas.

■ *Ralph Bakker*

THIERRY BONTRIDDER

Parure | 1994

56 X 40 X 0.3 CM

Titanium; hinged,
brushed texture, oxidized

PHOTO BY PAUL LOUIS

For me, *Blue Ring* represents the **pure freedom of design only accomplished with a mastery of the goldsmith's skills**. There is a spontaneity and lightness to this piece. I feel the sense of the gold being raised in the air; the ductility of the metal allowing the piece to be so thin it appears to float. ■ *Gina Pankowski*

BEATE KLOCKMANN
Blue Ring | 2002

4.5 X 4 X 4 CM

Gold, silver, enamel; hammered, milled, folded, soldered

PHOTO BY ARTIST

JENNIFER TRASK
Blue/Black Necklace | 2003

55.9 X 3.8 CM

18-karat gold, 22-karat gold, 24-karat gold, sterling silver,
lead, morpho butterfly wings, chrysomellidae, iron, pigments,
charcoal; fabricated, constructed, engraved

PHOTOS BY DEAN POWELL
COLLECTION OF THE MUSEUM OF ARTS + DESIGN, NEW YORK, NEW YORK

JULIE A. MATHEIS
Repose Collection: Cuffs | 2002
EACH, 0.2 X 7.5 CM IN DIAMETER
Feathers, thread; bound
PHOTO BY MARTY DOYLE

Keri Ataumbi is an artist I would like to learn more about. Her *Bird Hoops* convey the very essence of "bird" with an **absolute economy of line**. Their ear catch is gorgeous and simple. I am sure that they would be a pleasure to wear. ■ *Rebecca Hannon*

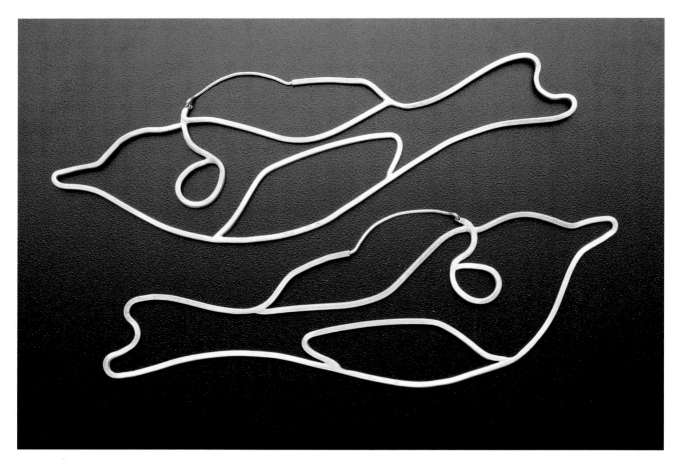

KERI ATAUMBI
Bird Hoops | 2006
EACH, 5.5 X 16 X 0.1 CM
Sterling silver; hand fabricated
PHOTO BY JOEL MULLER

These large rings **charge the space beyond their physical dimensions**. The iron contortions are redolent of fire dancers' or ribbon dancers' movements and refer me back to Alexander Calder's *Wire Circus*.

Beverley Price

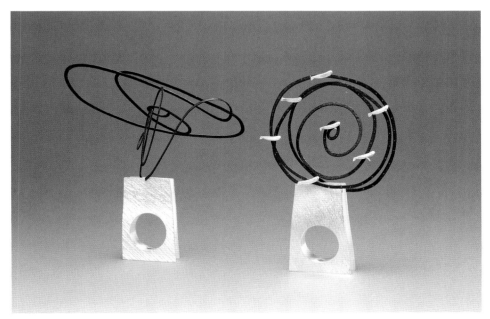

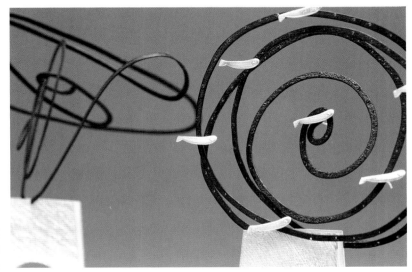

SUNGHO CHO
A Monument for the Sea | 2002
LEFT, 9 X 6.5 X 10 CM; RIGHT, 6 X 2.5 X 9.5 CM
Sterling silver, iron
PHOTOS BY MYUNG-WOOK HUH (STUDIO MUNCH)

Maria Phillips challenges nature itself in the creation of **wonder**. Through her commitment to craftsmanship, her unique approach to the discussion of nature versus culture, her **honesty** with material and technique, and her undeniable **intellect** and **intuition**, she infuses her work with tangible life and energy.

■ *Seth Papac*

MARIA PHILLIPS
Reminder #1 | 2003
11.4 X 2.5 X 5 CM
Copper, enamel, steel, silver,
18-karat gold, safety pin;
electroformed, fabricated, plated
PHOTO BY DOUG YAPLE

A **technical masterpiece** of the Old-World order. Freda has both skillfully and truthfully presented a self-contained narrative history.

■ *Lisa and Scott Cylinder*

DAVID C. FREDA

Study of Newborn White Crown Sparrows, Eggs, and Adults | 2001

22.9 X 14 X 3.8 CM

24-karat yellow gold, 18-karat yellow gold, fine silver, sterling silver, opals, enamel; hollow-core cast, fabricated, granulated

PHOTOS BY BARRY BLAU

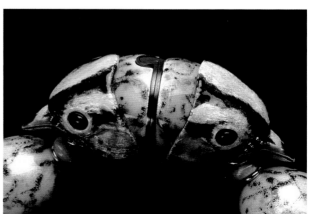

A seamless composition of many small parts that coalesce into an **animated figure full of humor**. Although the creature is large it sits over two fingers for comfort and stability; its knitted structure in small-scale wires makes it light despite its size. ■ *Arline M. Fisch*

REINA MIA BRILL
Giddey Up (double ring) | 2000
8.9 X 11.4 X 2.5 CM
Coated copper wire; hand knit
PHOTO BY ARTIST

Movement and calmness have rarely been brought into such delicate equilibrium. ■ *Beate Eismann*

DANIEL KRUGER
Untitled | 2004
7.5 X 7.5 X 3 CM
Copper, silk, 18-karat gold;
chased, forged, knotted
PHOTO BY NIKOLAUS BRADE

Shelley's rings are a **playful interpretation of the ordinary**, transforming them into the delightful and the extraordinary. ▪ *Nicole Jacquard*

SHELLEY NORTON
Untitled | 2001

VARIOUS DIMENSIONS

Monofilament, beads, sequins, plastic drink lid, sterling silver, semiprecious gemstones, 22-karat yellow gold; hand woven, bezel set

PHOTO BY JOHN COLLIE

It was very difficult to choose only a few pieces for this project. I found myself being drawn to the same artists' work over and over in each book. The work of Felieke van der Leest always made me linger a bit longer on the page because of the **playful nature** with which the subject is approached, the **wonderful texture**, and the seemingly **perfect color** combinations. ■ *Donna D'Aquino*

FELIEKE VAN DER LEEST
Stripey Animal Bracelets | 2003
EACH, 12.5 X 10 X 4.5 CM
Yarns, silver; crocheted, fabricated
PHOTO BY EDDO HARTMANN

This bracelet has a beautiful **natural form** made of a new **industrial material**. The spectrum of red colors makes it interesting. ■ *Miriam Verbeek*

CAROL-LYNN SWOL
Spirograph Bracelet, Red | 2004
12.7 X 10.8 X 5.7 CM
Tyvek, dye, sterling silver; cut, stacked, burned, soldered

LISA KLAKULAK
Untitled | 2007
21.6 X 14 X 3.2 CM

Wool fleece, black onyx cabochon,
glass seed beads, thread; dyed,
wet felted, hand stitched, beaded

COLD-WORKED BLOWN GLASS BY ETHAN STERN
PHOTOS BY STEVE MANN

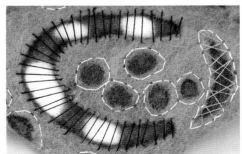

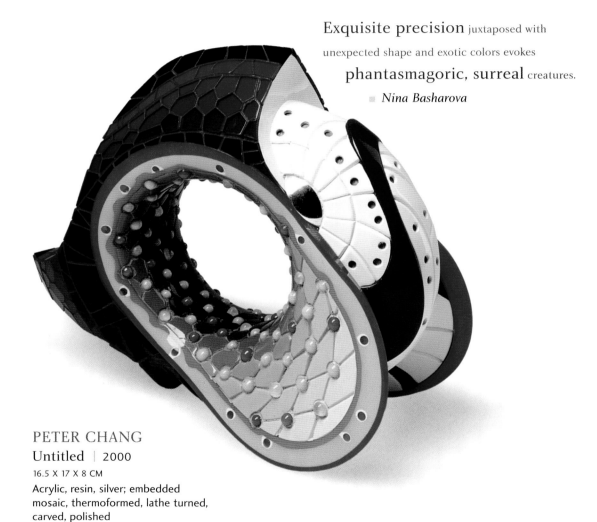

Exquisite precision juxtaposed with unexpected shape and exotic colors evokes phantasmagoric, surreal creatures.
■ *Nina Basharova*

PETER CHANG
Untitled | 2000

16.5 X 17 X 8 CM

Acrylic, resin, silver; embedded mosaic, thermoformed, lathe turned, carved, polished

PHOTO BY SHANNON TOFTS
PRIVATE COLLECTION

An impressive piece of work. Something to **cradle**, like a beautiful

pebble you find on the beach. ▪ *Suzanne Esser*

RUUDT PETERS
Azoth 6 Pyrit | 2004
LARGEST, 3.8 X 4.2 X 3.4 CM
Silver, polyester
PHOTO BY ROB VERSLUYS

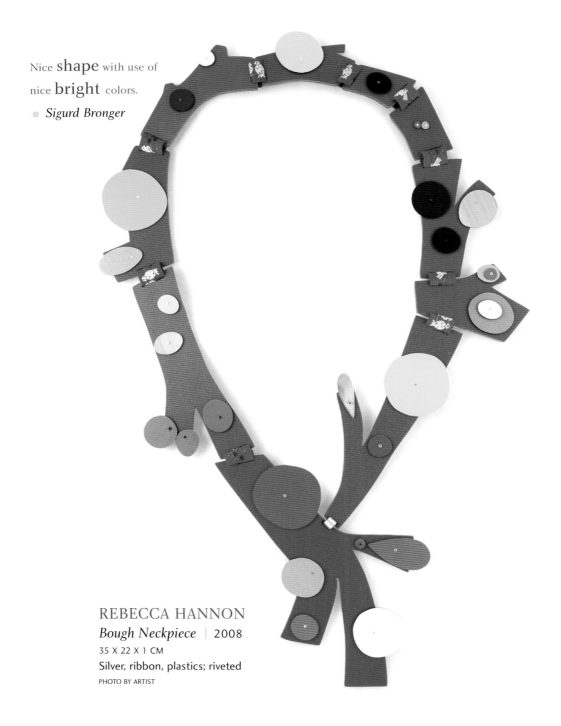

Nice **shape** with use of nice **bright** colors.
■ *Sigurd Bronger*

REBECCA HANNON
Bough Neckpiece | 2008
35 X 22 X 1 CM
Silver, ribbon, plastics; riveted
PHOTO BY ARTIST

At times I am drawn to work that has a vocabulary that relates to mine. At other times, I am fascinated by a piece of art where the artist does what I could never do. This is the case with the **poetic narrative** of Ramon's brooch. His approach is **intuitive**, and I can feel him playing with the design elements until they finally settle in their correct **composition**. In the end, every choice he makes seems right.   *Donald Friedlich*

RAMON PUIG CUYÀS
Reliquary | 2003
8.5 X 4.5 X 1.1 CM
Silver, nickel silver, wood,
plastic, found objects; assembled
PHOTO BY ARTIST

RAMON PUIG CUYÀS
From to Be Born the Wind | 2002
6.5 X 7 X 1 CM
Silver, nickel silver, wood, plastic,
glass, paper, cornaline; assembled
PHOTO BY ARTIST

I kept returning to the work of Ramon Puig Cuyàs and discovering something new each time. I enjoy his use of material and the way he combines his materials. To me, this work feels both **spontaneous** and **planned**.   *Donna D'Aquino*

Burcu Brooch innovatively transforms an everyday item. The folded, cross-sections of plastic drinking straws are almost unrecognizable. Instead, they become **colorful units of repetition**. Arranged and contained within a bold, concentric frame, I am reminded of the patterns within fruit. ■ *Anastasia Azure*

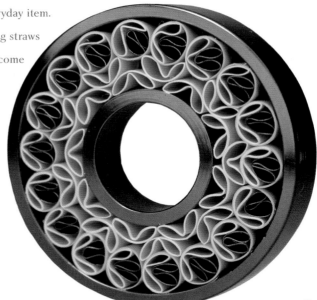

BURCU BÜYÜKÜNAL
Burcu Brooch | 2005
4 X 4 X 1 CM
Plastic drinking straws, thermoplastic, stainless steel, epoxy; lathe turned, assembled
PHOTO BY ARTIST

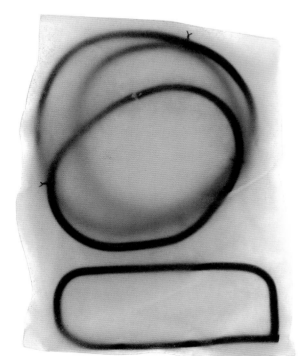

Transparency and color are its most evident features, while the internal elements play the main role. A very **poetic and emotional** graphic effect is created, with great **visual curiosity**.
■ *Fabrizio Tridenti*

COCO DUNMIRE
A Lightness | 2008
11.5 X 9 X 2 CM
Resin, pigment, silver, iron, steel; hammered, hand fabricated
PHOTO BY FEDERICO CAVICCHIOLI

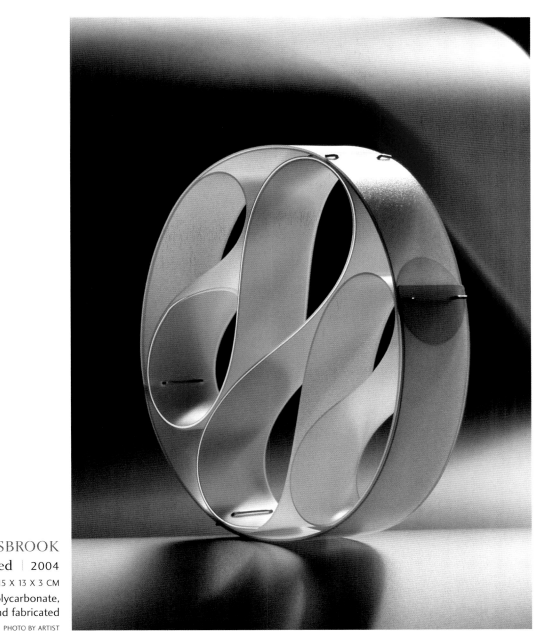

GILL FORSBROOK
Untitled | 2004
15 X 13 X 3 CM
Polypropylene, polycarbonate,
silver; hand fabricated
PHOTO BY ARTIST

TIM MCCREIGHT
Brooch | 2001
5.7 CM IN DIAMETER
Silver ingot; forged, chisel cut
PHOTO BY ROBERT DIAMANTE

ELIZABETH BONE
Moon Ring | 2001
6 CM WIDE
Silver; fabricated
PHOTO BY JOËL DEGEN

ARTHUR DAVID HASH
Puddle Series Bracelet | 2004
23 X 23 X 10 CM
Two-part plastic, dye
PHOTO BY ARTIST

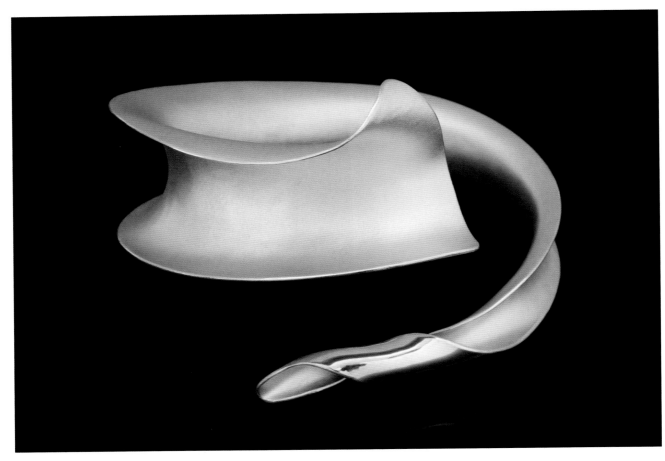

LORETTA TRYON
Satin Curve Cuff | 2008
6.5 X 2.5 X 7 CM
Sterling silver
PHOTO BY MICHAEL T. PYLE

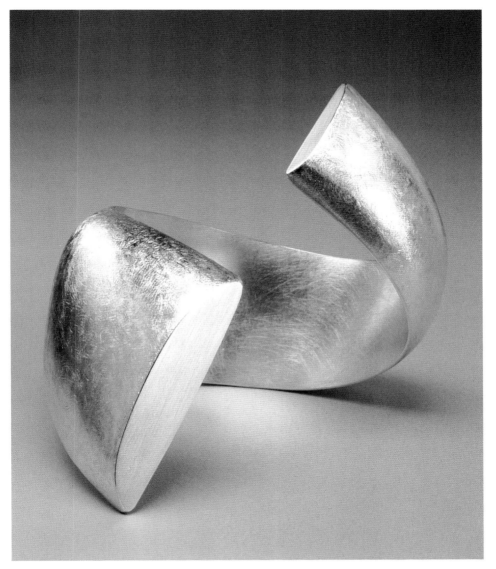

MONICA SCHMID

Sculpture Bracelet | 2004

11 X 8 X 9 CM

Sterling silver; forged,
hollow construction, fabricated

PHOTO BY PHILIP COHEN

There is so much **physical energy** accumulated in these pieces, and yet it appears so easily done. No soldering, just a piece of metal and raw physical power. If there is a profound difference between drilling and punching a hole, Michael knows it. He **masters metal** and displays it. It is **archaic** and **sophisticated** at the same time. ▪ *Castello Hansen*

MICHAEL CARBERRY
Series of Fine Silver Forged Rings | 2001–2002
EACH, 3.5 X 3.5 X 1.5 CM
Fine silver; forged
PHOTO BY JOËL DEGEN

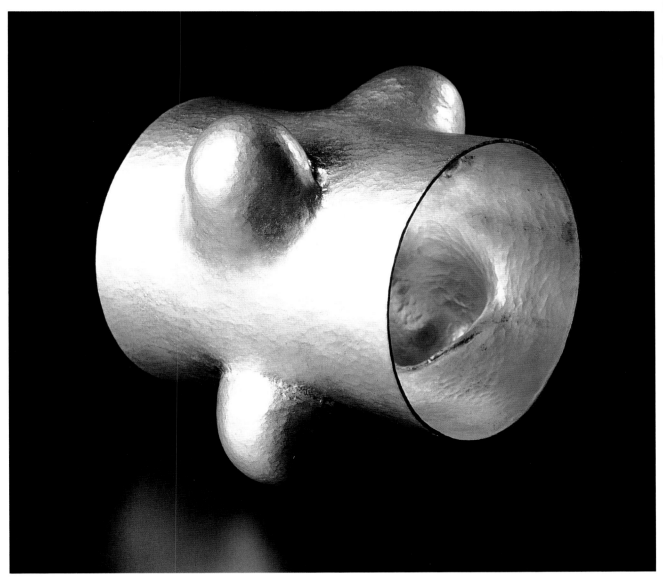

MIZUKO YAMADA
Tactile Bracelet | 2000
12 X 12 X 9 CM
Copper, silver; hammered, plated
PHOTO BY TOSHIHIDE KAJIHARA

Seemingly so simple in construction and design but **completely sophisticated** and very hard to pull off this well. A gorgeous piece. ■ *Mike Holmes*

SYBILLE RICHTER
Ansteckschmuck | 2003
4 X 8.5 X 6 CM
Sterling silver,
polyester resin; cast
PHOTO BY ARTIST

Mysterious, magical, and provocative. Hard silver metal was transformed into what appears to be soft human or animal skin. There is an element of secretiveness about the piece that makes the viewer feel as if he or she should not be looking at it. Yet, at the same time, one wants to stare at it and touch it, wondering what it is and how this **incredible transformation of material** took place. This wondrous, elegant form poses questions—an orifice is an opening, yet this form is folded and closed; an orifice on a human or animal is soft, yet this one is hard; an orifice sometimes has to do with our senses of smell and sight and this one relates to our sense of touch, making one want to feel it. How exciting to see and to wonder. ▪ *Marjorie K. Schick*

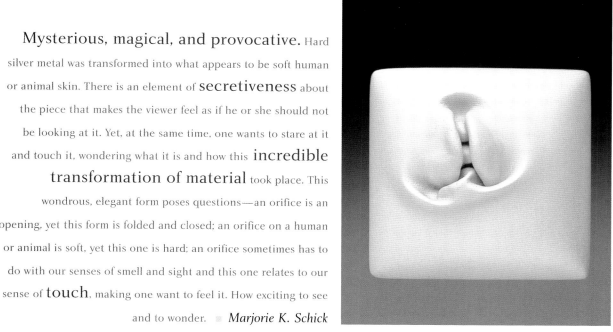

YUYEN CHANG
**Untitled Brooch
in the *Orifice* Series** | 2002
5.1 X 5.1 X 1.9 CM
Silver
PHOTO BY JIM WILDEMAN

ALESSIA SEMERARO
Untitled | 2002
4 X 2.5 X 1.5 CM
Cedar wood, metal, resin;
constructed, poured, burnt, coated
PHOTO BY FABIO VALENTI

JULIE BLYFIELD
Sliced Pod Brooches | 2003
EACH, 7.5 X 8.5 X 2.5 CM
Sterling silver; raised, cut, chased
PHOTO BY GRANT HANCOCK

YAEL KRAKOWSKI
Snake Bracelet | 2007
7.5 CM IN DIAMETER
Sterling silver, thread; hand
fabricated, oxidized
PHOTO BY ARTIST

Quietly bold, beautiful pieces.

■ *Deborrah Daher*

JOHANNA DAHM
Anti-Ashanti | 2002
3 X 2 CM
Fine silver; cast
PHOTO BY ARTIST

SALLY MARSLAND

almost black brooches | 2001–2003

3.5 TO 11.5 CM

Sterling silver, King William pine, ink, Paulonia (Chinese wood), textile dye, polyester resin, graphite, epoxy resin, slate, bone; oxidized

PHOTOS BY ARTIST

BEATE EISMANN
Steiger III | 2002
27 X 25 X 3.5 CM
Silver; cast, soldered, oxidized
PHOTO BY ARTIST

MANUEL VILHENA
Untitled | 2004
12 X 12 X 4 CM
Juniper wood, steel, pigment;
carved, assembled, dyed, waxed
PHOTO BY ARTIST

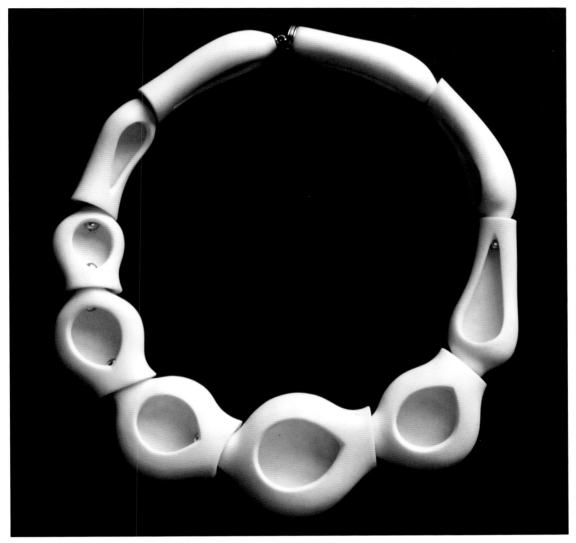

CHARLOTTE DE SYLLAS
Cacholong Necklace | 2005
160 X 16 X 2 CM
Cacholong, 18-karat gold
PHOTO BY JASPER VAUGHAN

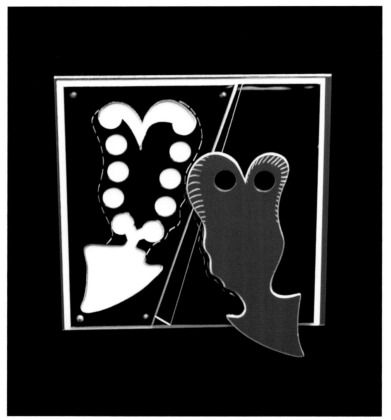

DAVID LAPLANTZ

Split Dichotomy Brooch | 1995

7 X 6.4 X 0.6 CM

Aluminum, iron; painted,
fabricated, riveted, engraved

PHOTO BY ARTIST

ABRASHA
Untitled | 1994
EACH, 3.8 X 1 CM
18-karat gold, stainless steel, platinum, diamonds; hand fabricated
PHOTO BY ARTIST

Luscious. ■ *Melanie Bilenker*

BRUCE METCALF
Shankless Plump Red Ring | 2003
3.8 X 5.7 X 2.5 CM
Gold-plated silver, wood; fabricated, carved, painted
PHOTO BY ARTIST

JOCELYN KOLB
Heliotroph | 2008
38 X 38 X 7.5 CM
Gypsum, epoxy resin;
3-D modeled, printed
PHOTO BY ARTIST

THE BEST OF THE 500 SERIES

CHARLES LEWTON-BRAIN
Untitled | 2001
EACH, 4 X 2.5 CM
18-karat gold;
fold formed, forged
PHOTO BY ARTIST

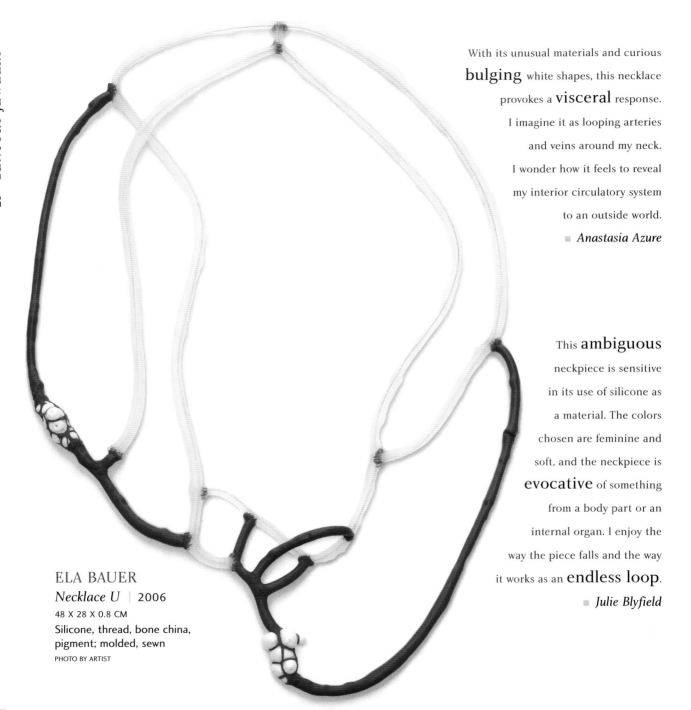

With its unusual materials and curious **bulging** white shapes, this necklace provokes a **visceral** response. I imagine it as looping arteries and veins around my neck. I wonder how it feels to reveal my interior circulatory system to an outside world.

■ *Anastasia Azure*

This **ambiguous** neckpiece is sensitive in its use of silicone as a material. The colors chosen are feminine and soft, and the neckpiece is **evocative** of something from a body part or an internal organ. I enjoy the way the piece falls and the way it works as an **endless loop**.

■ *Julie Blyfield*

ELA BAUER
Necklace U | 2006
48 X 28 X 0.8 CM
Silicone, thread, bone china, pigment; molded, sewn
PHOTO BY ARTIST

BRIDGET CATCHPOLE
Curiosities Series | 2006
EACH, 4 X 2 CM
Sterling silver, plastic from found object,
rubber; hand fabricated, oxidized
PHOTOS BY ANTHONY MCLEAN

A **humorous, playful** design.

— *Suzanne Esser*

CLAUDE SCHMITZ
Three Six One | 2006
19 X 19.5 X 1.8 CM
Onyx, silver, patina; constructed
PHOTO BY MARC WILWERT

The **perfection** of the craftsmanship and the associations of **frozen time** interest me in this piece. A childhood that now only exists in our minds?

■ *Hanna Hedman*

This object feels very **tender**; I wish to take it in my arms. The use of materials, the very sensitive and soft embedded toys, **like a dream** in a child's head, makes this work into a real artwork. ■ *Birgit Laken*

HYE WON KIM
Memento II | 2006
5 X 4 X 5 CM
Epoxy putty
PHOTO BY KWANG-CHOON PARK

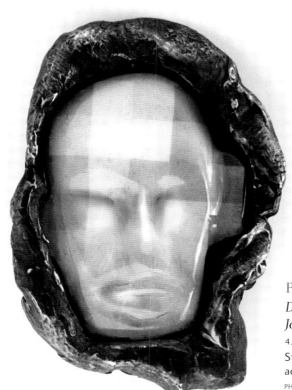

PETER DECKERS
Digital Division 3—
John van Neumann | 2001
4.3 X 3 X 0.6 CM
Sterling silver, digital print, acrylic; carved
PHOTO BY ARTIST

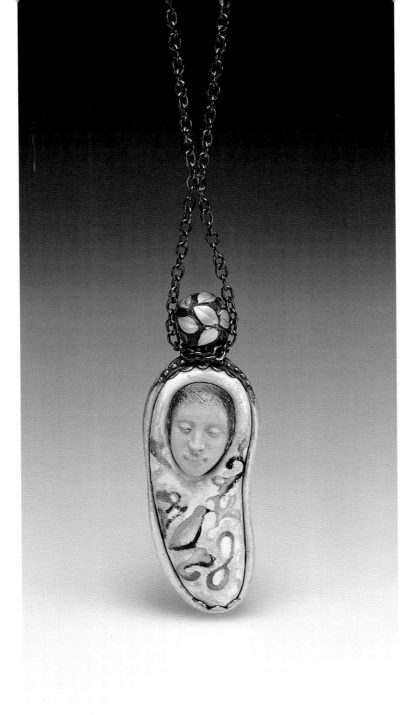

YEONMI KANG
Spring | 2003
PENDANT, 3.1 X 8.8 X 1.9 CM
Sterling silver, enamel,
24-karat gold; kum boo
PHOTO BY KWANG-CHOON PARK

Beautifully designed and executed, using contrasting materials and creating **superb elements of perspective**—and a kind of trompe l'oeil. ■ *Tom Muir*

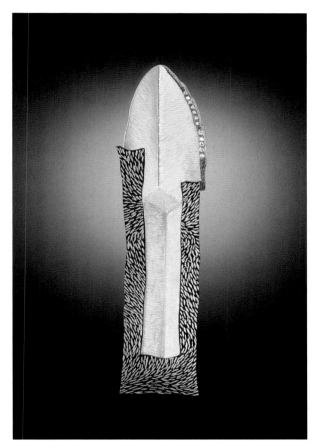

Like cat paws on water and heat waves shimmering in air, the strong inlaid colors and chiseled patterns create a **wonderful sense of motion** across the surface of this piece. Everything moves.

■ *George Sawyer*

NAMU CHO
Mirage 3-2 | 2004
8.9 X 3.2 CM
Damascene, 22-karat gold, diamonds
PHOTO BY HAP SAKWA

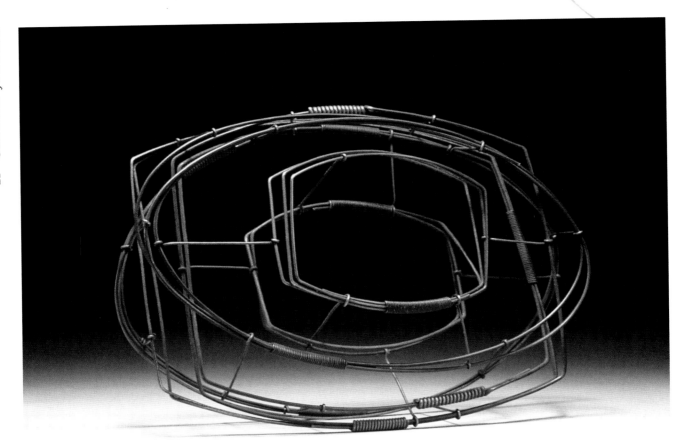

DONNA D'AQUINO
Wire Bracelet #83 | 2002
14 X 19.7 X 7.6 CM
Steel; hand fabricated
PHOTO BY ARTIST

Melanie's **idiosyncratic** approach to the historical use of hair in jewelry creates work that is both thoroughly **modern** and beautifully **reverent**. ▪ *Seth Papac*

Beyond the impressive technical achievement of contour drawing with hair, this locket captures a moment of **quiet solitude**. There's a **voyeuristic aspect** to the piece that I find interesting. ▪ *Jessica Calderwood*

MELANIE BILENKER
Clean Clothes ▏ 2007
4.5 X 4.8 X 1 CM
Gold, ebony, epoxy resin,
pigment, hair

PHOTO BY KEVIN SPRAGUE
CREATED WITH THE SUPPORT OF THE
PENNSYLVANIA COUNCIL ON THE ARTS

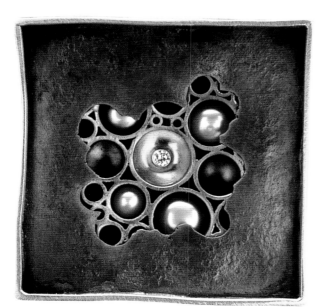

ANDY COOPERMAN
Royal Jelly ▏ 2000
4.4 CM WIDE
Bronze, sterling silver, 18-karat
gold, pearls, diamond; fabricated
PHOTO BY DOUGLAS YAPLE

JESSICA CALDERWOOD
Sleeping Beauties | 2007
5 X 6 X 0.5 CM
Enamel, copper, 18-karat gold,
brass, sterling silver, stainless steel
PHOTO BY ARTIST

A genius in his approach.

Machining becomes art.

■ *Michael Good*

WESLEY GLEBE
Finger Rings | 2003
VARIOUS DIMENSIONS
Titanium, 24-karat gold, stainless steel, platinum; cold connected
PHOTO BY MICHAEL BLACK

We love this piece for it's **powerfully simple forms** and the remarkable range of **tactile surfaces** that it contains. ■ *Jeff and Susan Wise*

SUSAN AND JEFF WISE
Kalahari Aurora | 2002
8 X 4 X 1 CM
Black jade, red coral, diamonds,
18-karat gold; carved, sculpted, inlaid
PHOTO BY ARTISTS

ANDREW L. KUEBECK
Trophy Locket | 2007

10 X 6 X 2 CM

Copper, enamel, photograph, velvet, amber;
fabricated, die formed, hung, stitched

PHOTO BY ARTIST

NATALYA PINCHUK
Growth Series: Brooch | 2007
14 X 7 X 5 CM
Wool, copper, enamel, plastic, waxed thread,
stainless steel; fabricated, assembled
PHOTO BY ARTIST

BARBARA COHEN

Cocoon & Fur Pendant | 2007

14 X 11 X 2.5 CM

Silk cocoons, sterling silver,
fox fur, paint; fabricated

PHOTO BY ARTIST

In this serious yet playful and **poetic** set of wedding rings, the entangled lines of metal represent the growing root system of the newlyweds. Two rings are **united** into one form to be worn simultaneously by two people. The choice of iron, an element found in the sun and the stars that represents **strength**, was appropriate for these rings. Just as the root system appears as if it can never be separated, the poignant accompanying verse about the rings is a part of the whole. This **symbolic root system** is a beautiful image, both in the photograph and in my mind. ■ *Marjorie K. Schick*

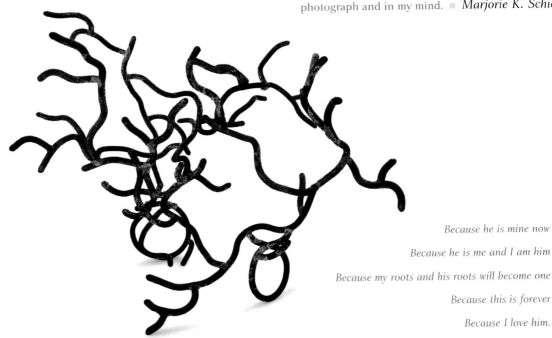

Because he is mine now
Because he is me and I am him
Because my roots and his roots will become one
Because this is forever
Because I love him.
Estela Saez Vilanova

ESTELA SAEZ VILANOVA
My Wedding Rings | 2006
11 X 15 X 10 CM
Iron
PHOTO BY ARTIST

DEBORAH LOZIER

Folded Flower Bracelet in Blue | 1999

11 X 11 X 2 CM

Enamel, copper; anticlastic raising,
welded, torch fired, fold formed

PHOTO BY ERIC SMITH

TINA RATH

Black Beauty: Sautoir 3 | 2004

3.5 X 3 X 120 CM

Ivory wood, 18-karat gold, mink, fox; carved, fabricated, felted

This necklace is elegant, classic, yet coming straight from the world of today. **Rules do not matter.** Spray paint is applied over 24-karat gold because that is what is needed to make the plump beads look luscious. **And why not, right?** ■ *Natalya Pinchuk*

ANYA PINCHUK
Necklace | 2004
19 X 19 X 2.5 CM
Sterling silver, 24-karat gold,
spray paint; plated
PHOTO BY ARTIST

WENDY MCALLISTER
Echinacea | 2009
8 X 8 X 4.5 CM
Sterling silver, copper mesh,
vitreous enamel; oxidized
PHOTO BY HAP SAKWA

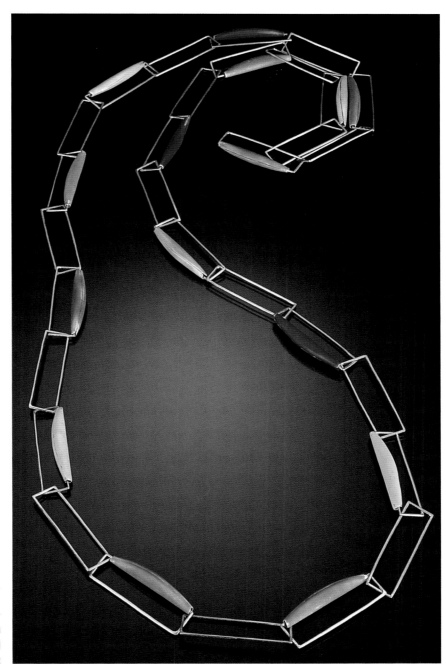

MARJORIE SIMON
Shades of Blue & Gold | 2004
LENGTH, 94 CM
Enamel, fine silver, 14-karat gold
PHOTO BY ROBERT DIAMANTE

The sharp edges of the petal-like shapes feel

warm and luminous. ■ *Namu Cho*

JAY SONG
Lantern | 2003
11.4 X 5 X 5 CM
Sterling silver, gold foil; fabricated
PHOTO BY TAWEESAK MOLSAWAT

I adore the **lacy organic feel** of this necklace. The colors of the metals and the stones complement each other perfectly.

■ *Joanna Gollberg*

An **exquisite abstraction** that recalls floral motifs without being obvious. The **rhythm, patterns, and colors** make for a beautiful and complete composition.

■ *Lisa and Scott Cylinder*

SUZAN REZAC
Necklace | 2007
0.5 X 48 X 5.5 CM
Sterling silver, coral, gold leaf:
oxidized, constructed, pierced
PHOTO BY TOM VAN EYNDE

BELLE BROOKE BARER
Aphrodite Cuff | 2008
7.5 X 7.5 X 7.5 CM
Sterling silver, 18-karat gold, cognac
diamonds; fabricated, oxidized
PHOTO BY GEORGE POST

The beauty is in the mix. The brooch has movement in its shape and gem placement, and then your eye focuses on the individual diamonds and sees the glorious mix of **colors, cuts, and forms**. Natural, raw diamonds play off the rose cuts so well, and you can revel in the glory of the natural color play from grey to green to red with countless shades in between. ■ *Cindy Edelstein*

TODD REED
Circular Rose-Cut Brooch | 2006
7.6 X 7 X 0.7 CM
Antique rose-cut diamonds, raw diamond cubes, 18-karat yellow gold, silver, patina; hand forged, fabricated
PHOTO BY ARTIST

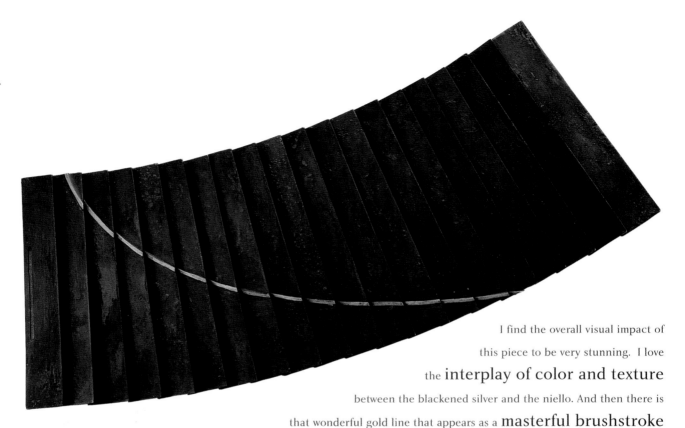

I find the overall visual impact of this piece to be very stunning. I love the **interplay of color and texture** between the blackened silver and the niello. And then there is that wonderful gold line that appears as a **masterful brushstroke** across the majority of the piece—its sparseness seems to speak volumes. ■ *Geoffrey D. Giles*

YOKO SHIMIZU
Untitled | 2004
7.5 X 20 CM
Silver, 24-karat gold, 18-karat gold; niello
PHOTOS BY FEDERICO CAVICCHIOLI

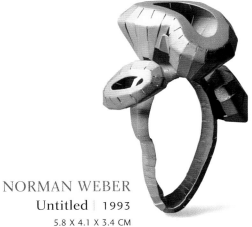

A very interesting approach to **metal as if it were paper**. More, we want more.

■ *Ralph Bakker*

NORMAN WEBER
Untitled | 1993
5.8 X 4.1 X 3.4 CM
8-karat gold; soldered
PHOTO BY ARTIST

I love the textural feel of this ring. I also **see the construction as it happened**, and it feels true rather than contrived. ■ *Joanna Gollberg*

YOKO SHIMIZU
Alone | 2002
4 X 2 X 2 CM
Oxidized sterling silver,
18-karat gold; constructed
PHOTO BY FEDERICO CAVICCHIOLI

Arty, but it works. Good sculptural shapes.

■ *Charlotte De Syllas*

HELFRIED KODRÉ

Amy | 1999

3.5 X 4.2 X 1.3 CM

Gold, white gold; soldered

PHOTO BY ARTIST

REIKO ISHIYAMA

Three Gold Panel Brooch | 2008

7 X 7 X 3.2 CM

Sterling silver, 22-karat gold leaf;
kum boo, fabricated, oxidized

PHOTO BY DAVID KATZ

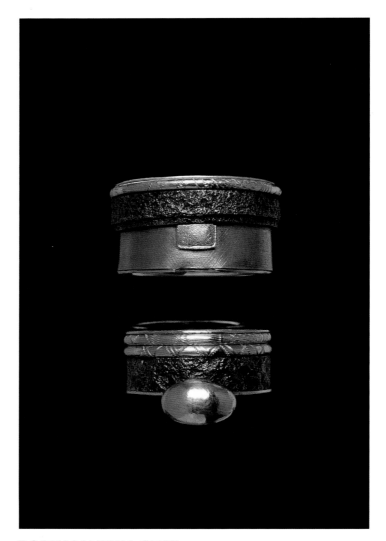

ROBIN MARTIN-CUST
Untitled | 1998
EACH, 1.9 X 1.9 X 1.3 CM
Found pitted steel, 18-karat
gold, nickel; fabricated
PHOTO BY KEN WOISARD

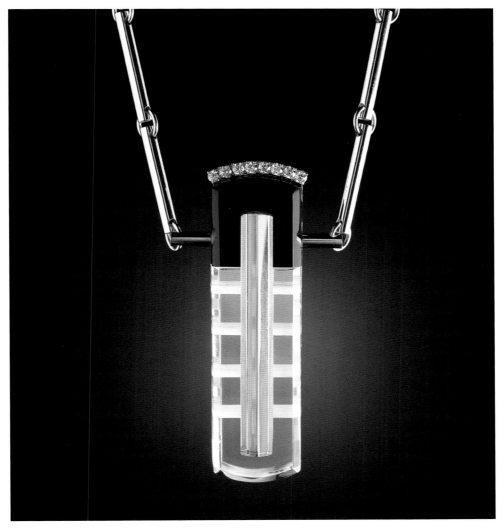

LINDA MACNEIL

Lucent Lines Necklace | 2005

5 X 2 X 1.3 CM

Vitrolite, clear glass, 14-karat white gold,
diamonds; polished

PHOTO BY BILL TRUSLOW

ROB JACKSON

Duomo | 1994

3.8 X 2.5 X 2.5 CM

Silver, 20-karat gold, topaz, garnets,
cameo shell; lost wax cast, fabricated,
carved, bezel set, tube set

PHOTO BY ARTIST

CAPPY COUNARD

Untitled | 2006

LEFT, 2.3 X 2.3 X 0.7 CM;
RIGHT, 2.2 X 2 X 0.7 CM

Sapphire, wrought iron,
18-karat gold; fabricated

PHOTO BY ARTIST

For me, it's a **beautiful combination** of metal
and diamonds. ■ *Tom Munsteiner*

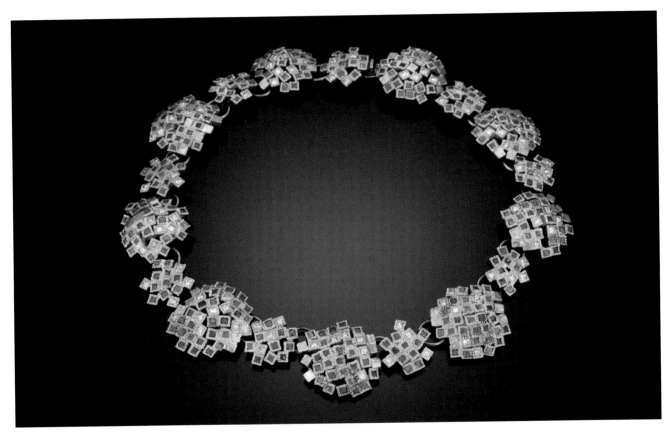

TODD REED
Diamond Cluster Necklace | 2004
2.5 X 0.6 X 43.2 CM
22-karat yellow gold, 18-karat yellow gold,
silver, diamonds; hand forged, fabricated
PHOTO BY AZAD

The lines in the quartz relate so nicely with the **formality** of the square and the rectangle in this pendant. The **facets** showing through the **translucent** stone add even more planar interest. ■ *Joanna Gollberg*

GEOFFREY D. GILES
Untitled | 2008
4.5 X 1.5 X 0.8 CM
18-karat palladium white gold, tourmalated quartz, diamonds; hand fabricated, bezel set, flush set, hand engraved
PHOTO BY ARTIST

Being able to **capture this special stone form** represents the skill of the artist. ■ *Tom Munsteiner*

JANIS KERMAN
Ring | 2002
3.2 X 1.9 CM
18-karat gold, aquamarine
PHOTO BY LARRY TURNER

The artist creates little treasures—**an intricate golden web of absolute complexity and precision**—through a traditionally precious medium and deceptively basic techniques. ■ *Nina Basharova*

GIOVANNI CORVAJA
Untitled | 2003
EACH, 3.2 X 3.2 X 1.2 CM
18-karat gold; soldered, niello
PHOTO BY ARTIST

In my eyes, this is an **absolutely perfect** craftsman's work. ■ *Tom Munsteiner*

GIOVANNI CORVAJA
Untitled | 2002
EACH, 3.2 X 3.2 X 0.3 CM
18-karat gold; granulation
PHOTO BY ARTIST

SEUNG-HEA LEE
Untitled | 2004
6.4 X 5.1 X 1.9 CM
18-karat gold, diamonds;
hand fabricated, bezel set,
satin finished
PHOTO BY MUNCH STUDIO

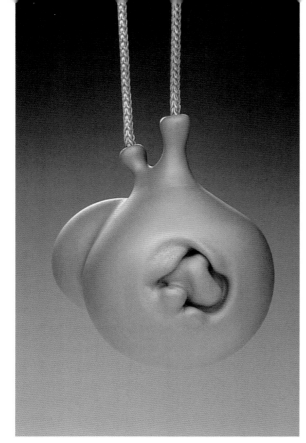

It is good to see someone using **raising techniques** in jewelry. The slow precision hammered forming combined with the **risk and thrill of the spontaneous**.

■ *Mary Lee Hu*

The artist has moved metal beyond its inherent properties, giving it the **illusion** of something **soft and pliable**. I enjoy the non-gender-specific **reference to the body** through the abstracted study of convex and concave form.

■ *Jessica Calderwood*

YUYEN CHANG
**Untitled Pendant
in the *Orifice* Series** | 2002
7.6 X 6.4 X 5.1 CM
Copper, copper plate, silver;
hand fabricated, hammered
PHOTO BY JIM WILDEMAN

Anthony Tammaro uses CAD/CAM technology to create interlocking, complex, and **sensual shapes evoking flesh and bone**. ■ *Anastasia Azure*

ANTHONY TAMMARO
Lattice Two | 2008
30 X 30 X 5 CM
Gypsum, epoxy resin, silicone rubber
PHOTOS BY ADAM WALLACAVAGE

PETER HOOGEBOOM
Mother Dao | 1995
5 X 52 X 2.5 CM
Ceramic, silver, brass
PHOTO BY TOM HAARTSEN

The way he uses the **vulnerable** ceramic in contemporary jewelry is quite unique. He casts special hollow components that feel **smooth** and make the jewelry relatively light. The texture and **rhythm** of the elements, the adding of a little color, and the little **stories** he tells with his work, are what really appeal to me.

■ *Ingeborg Vandamme*

Beautiful symbolic jewelry. The turtle as symbol for **long life** and the eggs for **fertility**. The smooth porcelain outside and the sensual red color inside of all the ceramic eggs are beautifully made. The chain is very rhythmic and **harmonious** like a good concert. ■ *Miriam Verbeek*

This is a beautiful gold ring because it has a lovely **rhythm** in its **understated design**. I would wear it every day if it belonged to me. It looks very comfortable. ■ *Daphne Krinos*

SUSAN MAY
Tall Ring | 2002
4 X 2.5 X 1.2 CM
18-karat gold; forged
PHOTO BY JOËL DEGEN

This piece feels like an expression of **time**. ■ *Deborrah Daher*

VANESSA SAMUELS
Layers #2 | 2003
2 X 2.5 X 0.5 CM
Beef bone, sterling silver;
carved, constructed, fabricated
PHOTO BY ARTIST

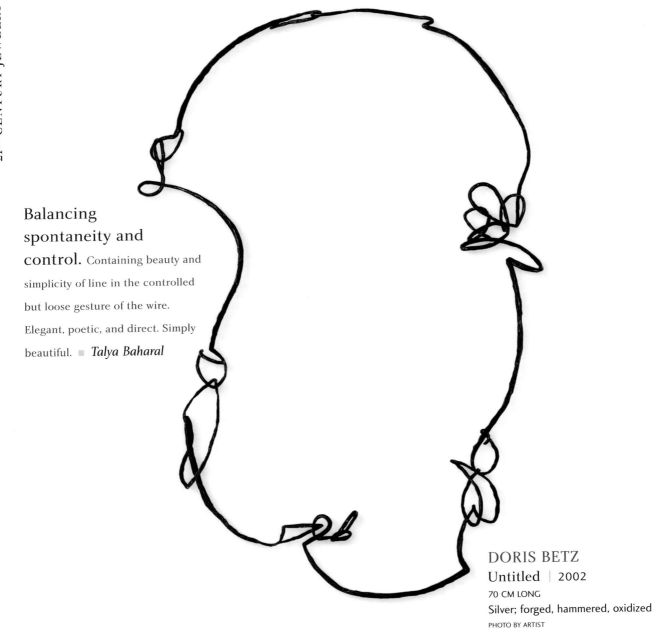

Balancing spontaneity and control. Containing beauty and simplicity of line in the controlled but loose gesture of the wire. Elegant, poetic, and direct. Simply beautiful. ■ *Talya Baharal*

DORIS BETZ
Untitled | 2002
70 CM LONG
Silver; forged, hammered, oxidized
PHOTO BY ARTIST

The wonderful feeling I get from this piece is so fragile and illuminating.

It's **bold** and **feminine** together. ▪ *Ruudt Peters*

I love the **strangeness** of his work, the
delicate use of color and odd shapes. It's very
poetic and ambiguous and makes me
wonder. ▪ *Katja Prins*

JAVIER MORENO FRIAS
Mesh | 2007
10.1 X 5.1 X 4 CM
Gold, silver, plastic,
paint; fabricated
PHOTO BY ARTIST

TOMOMI MATSUNAGA
Untitled | 2004
5 X 12 X 16 CM
Bamboo
PHOTO BY ARTIST

A well-made vessel. It offers me the raw material from which I start to contemplate **what has to be in this vessel**. ▪ *Ruudt Peters*

KARLA WAY
Material Worlds (Object to be Suspended) | 2008
11 X 7 X 7 CM
Thermoplastic, sterling silver, copper, enamel,
plastic, sand, epoxy resin, adhesive, paint,
cubic zirconia, silk cord, cotton; cold connected
PHOTO BY DOUGAL HASLEM

The concrete appears smashed, held together by **bonelike** silver bands that once may have been hidden within. What does it take to break you apart until your **insides are revealed?** ■ *Mia Maljojoki*

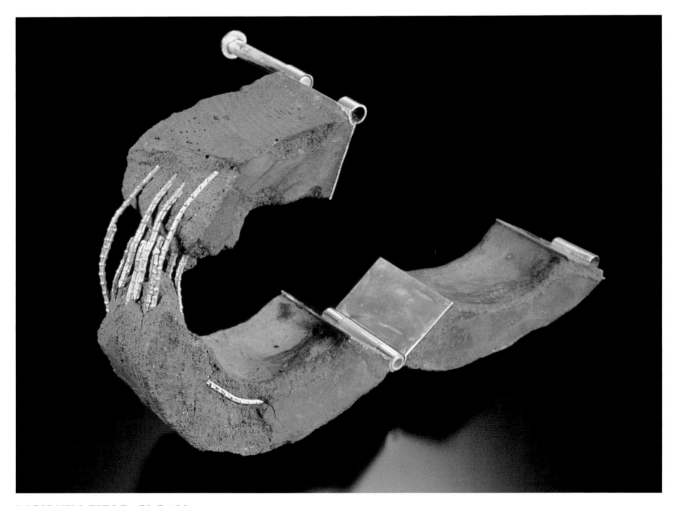

MCIRVIN FIELD-SLOAN
Crushing Me with Love | 2004
9 X 10.5 X 3.3 CM
Concrete, sterling silver; cast, hand fabricated
PHOTO BY ROBERT DIAMANTE

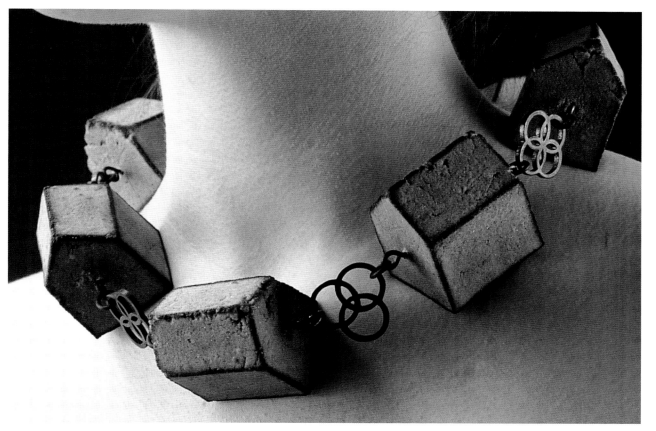

NISA BLACKMON
riveaux, redux | 2005

4.5 X 20.5 X 20.5 CM

Concrete, graphite, steel;
cast, burned, fabricated

PHOTOS BY ARTIST

Wood organically spirals around the wrist. **Was this grown or made?** ■ *Mia Maljojoki*

The wood has been carved, sawed, burned, and manipulated, leaving a very unique and **honest signature of the artist**. ■ *Charon Kransen*

FLÓRA VÁGI
Untitled | 2003
EACH, 4 X 10 CM IN DIAMETER
Wood, pigment, steel; hand fabricated, sawed, burned, riveted
PHOTO BY FEDERICO CAVICCHIOLI

With **simple actions**, sawing and burning, she gives a piece of wood a **new content** and suggests the natural wish of wearing this bracelet. ■ *Barbara Paganin*

Calling jewelry **monumental** does not always relate to scale. Rather, it can describe the conceptual, emotional, and sculptural significance of the form in space. This brooch asserts formidable **strength and restraint** in its design. ■ *Marthe Le Van*

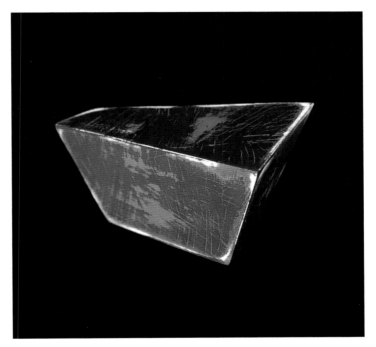

MIKE HOLMES

Brooch | 2003

8.9 X 6.4 X 5.1 CM

Walnut, gesso, gold leaf, pigments, brass, sterling silver; carved

PHOTO BY JEFFREY GOLDSMITH

Marcia was an artist with **clear sight**. Her voice could take **any form**— carved and painted wood, bold expressive silverwork, or a deep belly laugh at the absurdities of life. She is missed.

■ *Thomas Herman*

MARCIA A. MACDONALD
Left to right: Use the Internal Antennae, Stand Up For What You Believe In, Hollow Victories | 2003
EACH, 17.8 X 3.8 X 1.6 CM
Wood, paint, sterling silver, eggshell, thermoplastic, mica; carved
PHOTO BY HAP SAKWA

Lush, voluptuous plant and leaf forms beg to be caressed, yet subtly and protectively warn someone away with **forbidding thorns.** The wearer is transported—timeless green leafy woodland, the sound of cicadas, a midsummer bacchanal. Each component is **meticulously carved** from different woods and finished with attention to scale, volume, materials, and surface. The parts are joined with skillful metalsmithing techniques, allowing the necklace to be worn comfortably while complementing, even transforming, the wearer. ■ *Wendy McAllister*

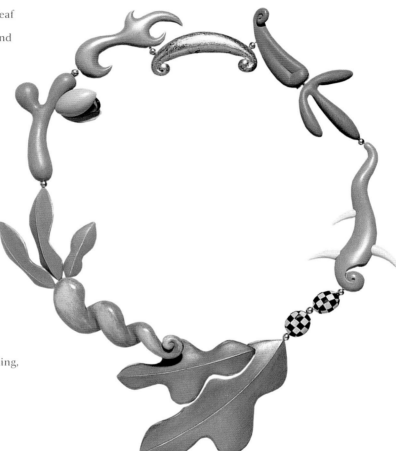

BRUCE METCALF
Green Leaf Necklace | 2003
35.5 X 30.5 CM
Maple, ebony, holly, brass, 24-karat gold, paint; carved, machined, fabricated, plated
PHOTO BY ARTIST

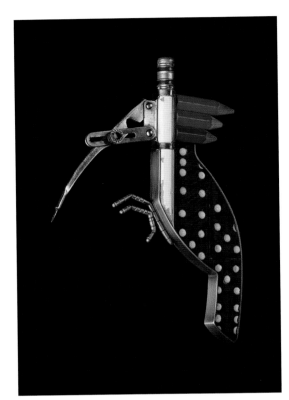

LISA AND SCOTT CYLINDER

Pencilated Woodpecker Brooch | 2004

12.7 X 7.6 X 0.6 CM

Sterling silver, brass, compass, antique wooden dominoes, pencils, epoxy resin; formed, fabricated

PHOTO BY JEFFREY K. BRADY

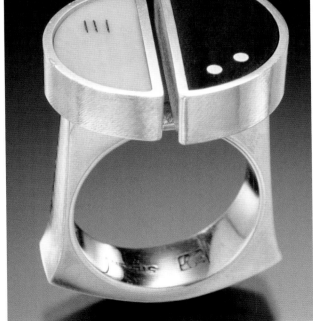

KRISTIN MITSU SHIGA

Modernismus I | 2002

2.5 X 2.2 X 2.2 CM

Sterling silver, ebony, piano key ivory; scrimshaw, cast, fabricated

PHOTO BY HAP SAKWA

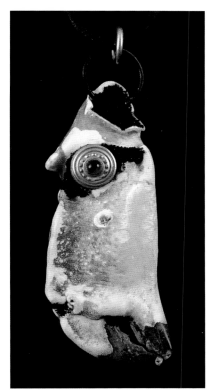

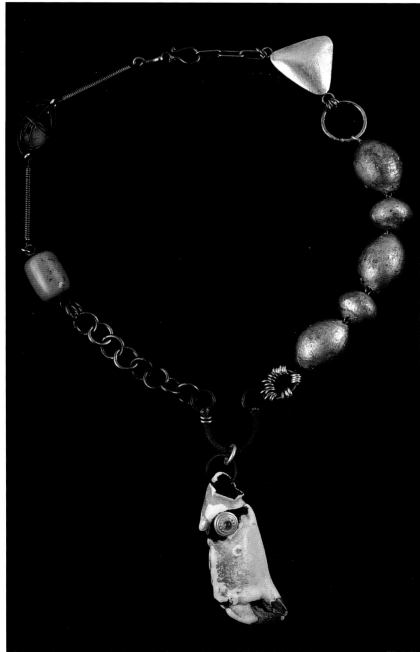

ROBERT EBENDORF
Gold Eye Necklace | 2004

LENGTH, 63.5 CM

Wood, 24-karat gold foil, amber, crab claw, iron wire, silver, 24-karat gold, ruby

PHOTOS BY TIM LAZURE

The corn was processed with the sense that, **as a material, it has everything one could wish for** with regard to shape and aesthetics. The effect of this piece is **archaic,** relating to traditional jewelry dating back thousands of years, yet it still seems **astonishingly modern.** ■ *Beate Eismann*

BRIAN ROBERTS
Baby Blue | 2002
11.5 X 11.5 X 3.8 CM
Blue popcorn, steel; carved, riveted
PHOTO BY JEFFREY SABO

This piece has great **humor and playfulness**. I appreciate the reference to the prized "deer rack" as it moves from the wall to the body and is literally turned on its head. ∎ *Jessica Calderwood*

FELIEKE VAN DER LEEST
Camouflage Deer with Target Pants | 2003
DEER, 12 X 12 X 6 CM
Rubber, gold, coral, pearl, textile; crocheted, constructed, cast
PHOTOS BY EDDO HARTMANN

Although only an inch tall, you feel the seemingly **great weight** of this beautifully modeled creature hoisted by silver chains around your neck.

■ *Mike Holmes*

KATHLEEN R. PRINDIVILLE
Hippo | 2006
3 X 4 X 1 CM
Sterling silver, white bronze, patina; cast, molded
PHOTO BY MARTY DOYLE

JANE DODD
Rabbit Leuchterweibchen Brooch | 2007
6 X 6.3 X 1.2 CM
Sterling silver, sapphire, ebony
PHOTO BY HARU SAMESHIMA

I caught my breath when turning this page, because seeing David's *Pink Snail* is like seeing an old friend. I have touched and worn this brooch in real life. It embodies all the excellent qualities of David's work, such as his **intense research into everyday materials**, revealing a whimsical translation into a perfect piece of jewelry. ▪ *Rebecca Hannon*

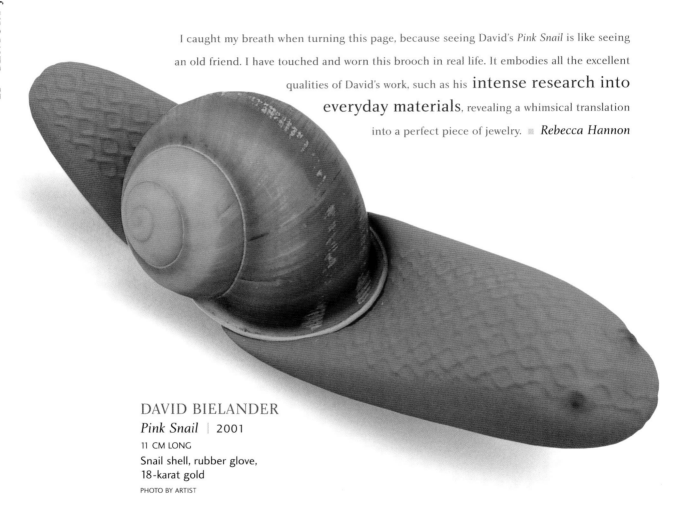

DAVID BIELANDER
Pink Snail | 2001
11 CM LONG
Snail shell, rubber glove,
18-karat gold
PHOTO BY ARTIST

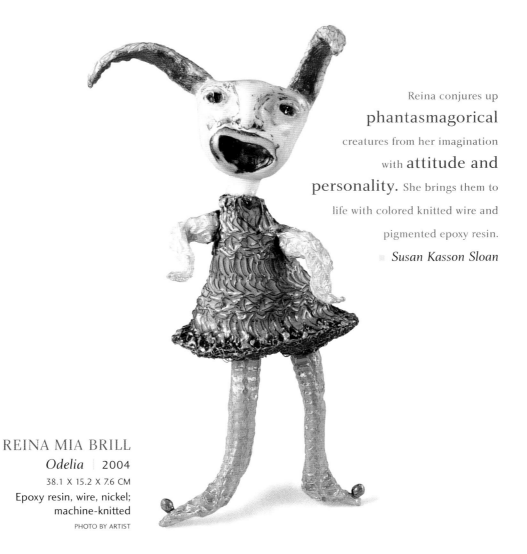

Reina conjures up
phantasmagorical
creatures from her imagination
with **attitude and
personality.** She brings them to
life with colored knitted wire and
pigmented epoxy resin.

■ *Susan Kasson Sloan*

REINA MIA BRILL
Odelia | 2004
38.1 X 15.2 X 7.6 CM
Epoxy resin, wire, nickel;
machine-knitted
PHOTO BY ARTIST

257

To stumble across such a scrap of plastic and see this piece of jewelry in it is like finding a **diamond in the dumpster**. ■ *Felieke van der Leest*

NICOLE LEHMANN
Brooch | 2008
6.5 X 12 X 1 CM
Found plastic fragment,
14-karat gold; assembled
PHOTOS BY ARTIST

Original and poetic.

■ *Sigurd Bronger*

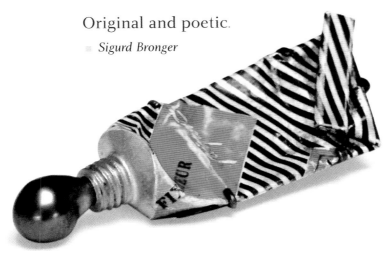

BERNHARD SCHOBINGER
Pearl out of the Tube | 2002
6.9 X 1.7 X 0.9 CM
Tahitian pearl, chromium,
aluminum tube, paint; printed
PHOTO BY P. VOELLMY

These rings bring back **memories** of the **excitement** of traditional Korean kite-fighting festivals.

■ *Namu Cho*

JAY SONG
Kites (set of ten) | 2002
VARIOUS DIMENSIONS
Sterling silver, gold foil, oil paint; fabricated
PHOTO BY TAWEESAK MOLSAWAT

The most **outrageous** ring I have ever seen—**full bodied** and **feather light** at the same time. ■ *Felieke van der Leest*

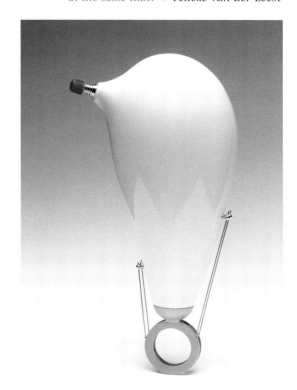

SIGURD BRONGER
Ring | 1996
13 X 3 CM
Steel, silver, hard foam, lacquer
PHOTO BY ARTIST

Creating brooches
from earplugs is
**pleasing to the
fingertips**.

■ *Ruudt Peters*

JIRO KAMATA
Tsubomi | 2003
LARGEST, 6 X 6 X 3 CM
Ear plugs, silver; oxidized
PHOTOS BY ARTIST

EMIKO OYE

Tire Earrings | 2006

EACH, 5.8 X 2.4 X 1.4 CM

Rubber, plastic, cubic zirconia,
14-karat gold, sterling silver; hand fabricated

PHOTO BY HAP SAKWA

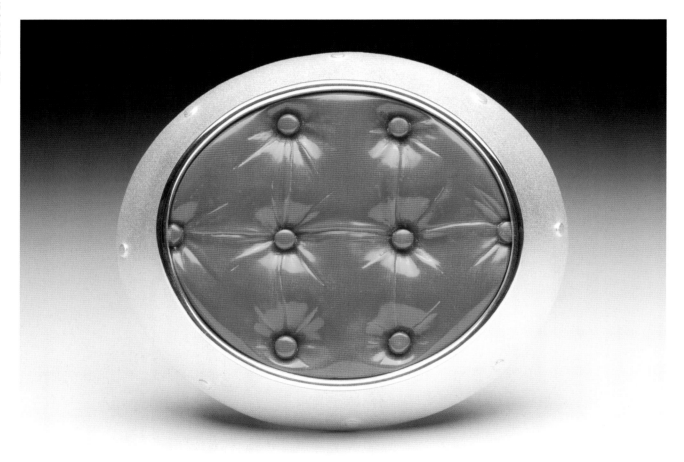

DIANE FALKENHAGEN
Red Upholstery Brooch | 2008
6.7 X 8.3 X 1.9 CM
Sterling silver, acrylic polymer;
fabricated, carved
PHOTO BY BILL POGUE

I wish I had owned this bracelet when I was in my **heavy metal period!**

■ *Felieke van der Leest*

This bracelet makes playful use of a rubber tire from a toy truck, but the **graphic**, matte black tread, combined with the **smooth** brushed silver core, results in a thoroughly **sleek** and **modern** piece.

■ *Ann L. Lumsden*

JULIA TURNER
Monster Truck Series #1 | 2001
11 X 11 X 7 CM
Rubber toy truck tire,
sterling silver; fabricated
PHOTO BY ARTIST

I am drawn to the **unexpected** in art and appreciate the **transformation of the everyday**, mundane materials like these sticky notes into a fabulously textured, playful, and **temporary** cuff. ■ *emiko oye*

TING-TING TSAO
MEMO II | 2004
15 X 6 X 3.5 CM
Self-adhesive notes; written, hand fabricated
PHOTO BY KAREN LUNG TSAI

Cynthia Toops takes industrial tape and **transforms** it into a bracelet of unexpected form and dimension. She exemplifies the artist's role to take an **ordinary** material and transform it into something **extraordinary**. ■ *Harriete Estel Berman*

CYNTHIA TOOPS
Untitled Cuff Bracelet | 2006
10 X 10 X 4 CM
Industrial insulating tape, spring; hand cut, hole punched
PHOTO BY ROGER SCHREIBER

HARRIETE ESTEL BERMAN
Bead Embellishment Bracelets | 2004
LARGEST, 17.8 CM
Pre-printed steel from recycled containers,
plastic core; hand fabricated, pinked,
hydraulic press formed
PHOTO BY PHILIP COHEN

BORIS BALLY
Scrap Leaves: B Wear | 2005
66 X 36 X 16 CM
Recycled traffic signs, steel cable,
key rings; hand fabricated
PHOTO BY AARON USHER III
MODEL, DOMINGO MONROE

I imagine wearing this colorful, graphic, and playful bracelet to an **intergalactic cocktail party**. The organic tendrils reach toward an architectural edge.

■ *Anastasia Azure*

PETER CHANG
Untitled Bracelet | 2005
15.3 X 15.3 X 5.2 CM
Acrylic, PVC, found plastic,
silver; thermoformed, carved,
lathe turned, polished
PHOTO BY ARTIST

This has been one of my favorite pieces of jewelry for many years. It's such a simple idea, beautifully rendered, and about as **sensual** as any jewelry I've ever seen. **Luscious**. I don't know whether to **eat it** or **wear it**, but I do know **I want it**.

Donald Friedlich

DANIEL JOCZ
Cherry Solitaire | 1999
5.7 X 2.2 X 2.2 CM
Enamel, copper, 18-karat
gold; repoussé
PHOTO BY DEAN POWELL

FRITZ MAIERHOFER
Wedding Rings for Aloha and Anatol | 2006
EACH, 1 X 2 CM
Acrylic, platinum
PHOTO BY ARTIST

The jewelry of Daniel Kruger is fascinating because of its **authentic language** and high craftsmanship. The **sensibility** and **sensuality** in his works cannot leave one untouched.

Claude Schmitz

DANIEL KRUGER
Untitled | 2003
8 X 9 X 4 CM
Sterling silver, turquoise chips,
coral; forged, hinged, knotted
PHOTO BY NIKOLAUS BRADE

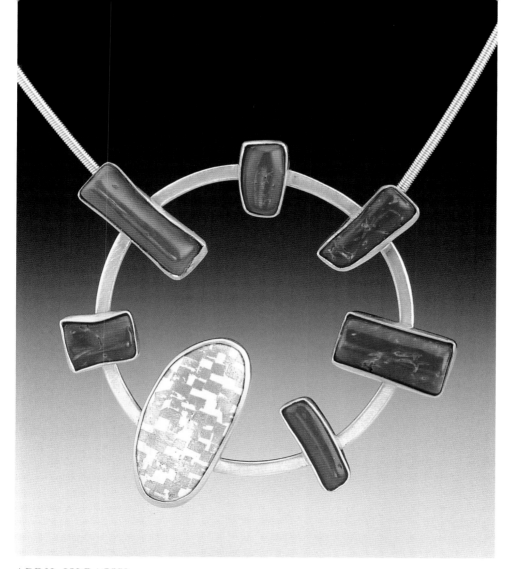

APRIL HIGASHI

Constellation II Pendant | 2004

8 X 8 X 1 CM

24-karat gold, 22-karat gold,
18-karat gold, coral, enamel; fabricated

PHOTO BY HAP SAKWA

With this **enigmatic object**, presented as a ring, Peters asks the wearer to **consciously grasp a mystery**, and to take control of the "reveal" by how we would choose to wear it. I am intrigued by how either **nature** (the desert rose rock) or **technology** (the altered vessel) will be obscured, or presented, on opposite sides of the same hand. ■ *Nisa Blackmon*

RUUDT PETERS

Ouroboros, Mibladen | 1994

3 X 4 X 6 CM

Silver, desert rose, paint

PHOTO BY ROB VERSCUYS

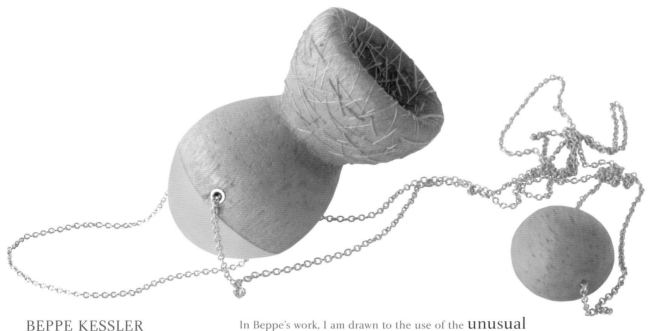

BEPPE KESSLER

Heritage | 2005

5 X 2 X 2 CM

Gold, silver, alabaster, balsa wood, cotton

PHOTO BY ARTIST

In Beppe's work, I am drawn to the use of the **unusual** materials, the **subtle** changes of color, and the **delicate** texture created from the stitching. ■ *Nicole Jacquard*

SUZANNE ESSER
Brooch | 2008
10 X 5.5 X 1.2 CM
Sterling silver, sand,
patina; oxidized
PHOTO BY ARTIST

ADREAN BLOOMARD
Oplontis Collection-OP3412 | 2006
6 X 3.5 X 2 CM
18-karat gold, crushed turquoise; constructed
PHOTO BY FILIPPO VIRARDI

The scale, material, and structure of the gold surface make the bracelet refined and **timeless**. Here, the order of the construction meets the free morphology of the gold plates. Holes grant a sort of **mysterious** nature to this jewelry.

■ *Pavel Herynek*

STEFANO MARCHETTI
Untitled | 2003
7 X 7 X 9 CM
18-karat gold
PHOTO BY ROBERTO SORDI

What I love about this brooch is that it is as if the gemstones are **exploding** away from the central circle, and the only thing keeping them from flying away are the claw settings. As a result, the piece holds a wonderful **visual tension**.

■ *Geoffrey D. Giles*

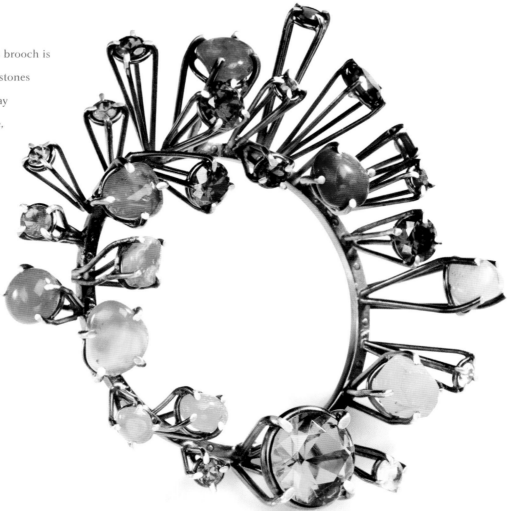

JOANNA GOLLBERG
Reds to Yellow Brooch | 2008
7.6 X 7.6 X 3.2 CM
Sterling silver, semiprecious stones;
fabricated, oxidized, faceted
PHOTO BY STEWART O'SHIELDS

The **tactile** and **modular** qualities of this

bracelet invite you to wear it.

■ *Claude Schmitz*

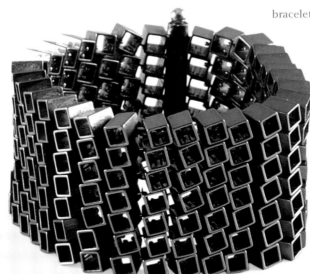

SALIMA THAKKER

Modular Bracelet 2 | 2003

4.5 X 18 X 0.7 CM

18-karat yellow gold, sterling silver,
patina; hand fabricated

PHOTO BY PHOTOLOGY

The ring has an aesthetic character that can be defined as **historical**. It represents a recognizable model from a great period in jewelry, which still has a **strong influence** on the new generations of artists. ■ *Stefano Marchetti*

HERMANN JÜNGER

Helen's Ring | 1990

Gold, opal, chrysoprase, emerald, tourmaline, rough diamond, sapphire

PHOTO BY EVA JÜNGER
COLLECTION OF THE MUSEUM OF FINE ARTS, HOUSTON, TEXAS

JASMIN WINTER
Friends of Mine: Two Sides | 2009
63 CM LONG
Sterling silver, enamel, resin,
thread; annealed, oxidized
PHOTO BY CAROLIN MÜLLER

I know it seems vain to select my own work, but it is one of those pieces that just **grabs my attention**.

■ *Nanz Aalund*

NANZ AALUND
Two-Finger Wedding Band | 2005

2.7 X 4.1 X 0.3 CM

Platinum, sterling silver, 24-karat gold, diamond; cast, fabricated

PHOTO BY JIM FORBES

SEAN AND SCOTT WEAVER
Large Boat Earring | 2005

EACH, 4 X 1 X 1.8 CM

18-karat gold, diamonds; hand fabricated

PHOTO BY HAP SAKWA

LANELLE W. KEYES
Hercules Knot | 2002
7.5 X 7.5 X 3 CM
Iron, 18-karat gold;
hand knitted, knotted
PHOTO BY DOUG YAPLE

There are artists who, once they become famous, repeat their aesthetic model for their entire careers. Others, like Giampaolo Babetto, prefer methodically **questioning** themselves, **changing and risking**, uninterruptedly, what they present to the public despite the success they have achieved. ▪ *Stefano Marchetti*

GIAMPAOLO BABETTO
Untitled | 2002
3.7 X 2.8 X 2.9 CM
18-karat yellow gold, pigment
PHOTO BY LORENZO TRENTO

Complicated and simple at the same time.

Beautiful construction. ■ *Sigurd Bronger*

Constructed and translated from a simple line drawing into a bracelet with a **refined form**. Only adding what makes the form stronger and more complex.

■ *Charon Kransen*

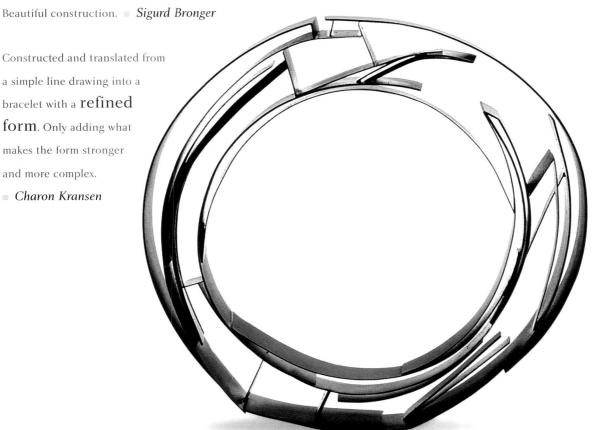

MARI FUNAKI
Untitled | 2004
9.2 X 8.9 X 1.1 CM
Mild steel; heat colored, fabricated
PHOTO BY TERENCE BOGUE

The graphic pattern and the transparent, milky effect of the chains' connections have a simple and perfect beauty, creating a **very special and intelligent** piece of jewelry. ■ *Andrea Wagner*

I like the **simplicity** of the rings combined with the use of the knot as a symbol for **eternity**. ■ *Gurhan Orhan*

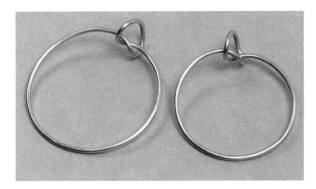

TRACY STEEPY
Both | 2006
80 X 28 X 1 CM
Acrylic polymer, sterling silver, epoxy resin; fabricated, laser cut, inlaid, hand drawn
PHOTO BY ARTIST

DIANA DUDEK
Untitled | 2004
LEFT, 2 X 2.5 X 1 CM;
RIGHT, 1.8 X 2 X 1 CM
18-karat gold
PHOTO BY ARTIST

These earrings are a very good study on form and its wearability. ▪ *Leonor Hipólito*

JIRO KAMATA
Cube | 2005
EACH, 2 X 2 X 2 CM
18-karat gold
PHOTOS BY ARTIST

CYNTHIA EID

Knot | 1985

2.5 X 2.2 X 0.5 CM

14-karat yellow gold;
wax worked, cast

PHOTO BY ARTIST

This neckpiece is an astonishing 1970s masterwork by the late William Clark. The hand-raised, double-spiral tapered tube is a **technical tour de force**, but the complex form manages to be both **celebratory** and **elegant**. I had the good fortune to wear this piece, and it was a delightful experience. You don't wear it, it wears you. ▪ *Mike Holmes*

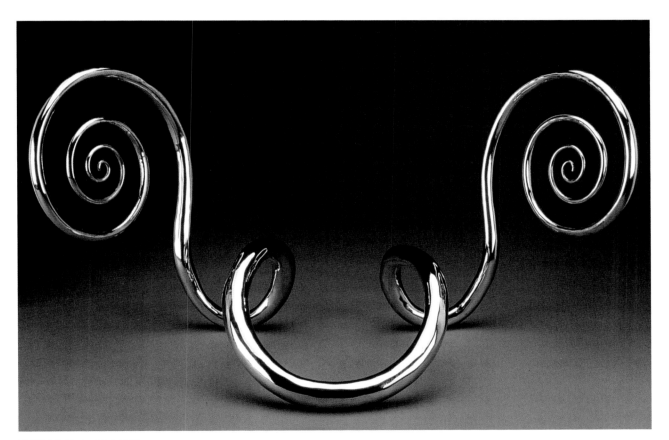

WILLIAM CLARK
Spiral Dancepiece | 1975
55 X 71 X 32 CM
Yellow brass; hand forged
PHOTO BY RICHARD SARGEANT

JAYNE REDMAN
Columbine Earrings | 2003
EACH, 4.2 X 2 X 2 CM
18-karat yellow gold, 18-karat
white gold, sterling silver; hand
fabricated, oxidized
PHOTO BY ROBERT DIAMANTE

LOLA BROOKS
32 filigree balls | 2005

9 X 16 X 9 CM

Champagne rose-cut diamonds,
stainless steel, 18-karat gold,
18-karat solder; fabricated

PHOTO BY DEAN POWELL
PRIVATE COLLECTION

I chose this bold necklace because it
embraces its tremendous jewelry heritage
while at the same time flirts with conventions.

Mary Hallam Pearse

The graphic style of this work is like a playful **sketch** caught in metal. I like the suggestion of **space** and the combination of the materials: the **lively contrast** between the blackened silver and the shiny gold. These earrings make me think of the beach, when the sea leaves shells behind in layers of sand and water. Natural elements like shells, the true treasures, were more valuable than precious stones for me when I was a child, and they still are. These earrings reflect that idea. ■ *Ingeborg Vandamme*

BIBA SCHUTZ

Lacy Loops | 2005

EACH, 4.4 X 4.4 X 1.8 CM

Sterling silver, 22-karat gold;
cast, forged, hand fabricated, oxidized

PHOTO BY RON BOSZKO

PAT FLYNN
Trifold Cuff | 2008
3.7 X 6.3 X 5.7 CM
Iron, 22-karat gold, 18-karat gold, platinum,
diamonds; forged, fused, fabricated
PHOTO BY HAP SAKWA

Decoration, chaos, and order in one. ■ *Ruudt Peters*

HELEN BRITTON
Pink Garden | 2003
4 X 3 X 3 CM
Paint, silver
PHOTO BY ARTIST

HANNA HEDMAN
What You Tell Is Not Always What
You Have Experienced | 2009
56 X 23 X 14 CM
Sterling silver, copper, paint;
oxidized, forged, powder coated
PHOTO BY SANNA LINDBERG

Red and precious, like an exotic coral necklace, but **delicious and homely**, like a carrot soup. ■ *Barbara Paganin*

JUN WON JUNG
Carrot | 2005
2.5 X 27.5 X 27.5 CM
Carrot, stainless steel wire
PHOTO BY KWANG-CHOON PARK

LIN STANIONIS
Untitled Brooch | 2008
10.2 X 10.2 X 1.9 CM
Urethane resin; cast
PHOTO BY JON BLUMB

Leather fingers **referencing the hand** where it will be worn. It is as if the human body is being used to decorate itself. **Who is wearing whom?** ■ *Mia Maljojoki*

INEKE HEERKENS
Beweging | 2001
5 X 15 X 12 CM
Leather, hook-and-loop tape
PHOTO BY EDDO HARTMANN

This ring develops the impossible connection between metal, an eternal and **immutable** material, and vegetable, a **perishable** and transforming item. A concept that opens up worrying scenarios on the eternal **duality of life and death**. A ring that cannot be worn, but it will lead to thinking about the value of **freedom and time**. ■ *Fabrizio Tridenti*

HILDE DE DECKER
For the Farmer and the Gardener | 1997–2003
VARIABLE DIMENSIONS
Silver, vegetables
PHOTO BY ARTIST

Relationships are often built from local occasions. Here we see that the linkage to the earth relates well to the marriage liturgy "Till Death Do Us Part." The fragility of the material covers formation and solidity, but also disintegration and temporality. The image summarizes well, how "marriages" come and go. ■ *Peter Deckers*

RENEÉ ZETTLE-STERLING
Cherished Rings, Cherished Earth | 2006
LEFT, 3.8 X 3.2 X 1.3 CM; RIGHT, 3.2 X 3.2 X 1.3 CM
Compressed earth; cut
PHOTO BY ARTIST

Ephemeral like a wedding day
everlasting like a glacier
delicate like a marriage
lovely like my love

Barbara Paganin

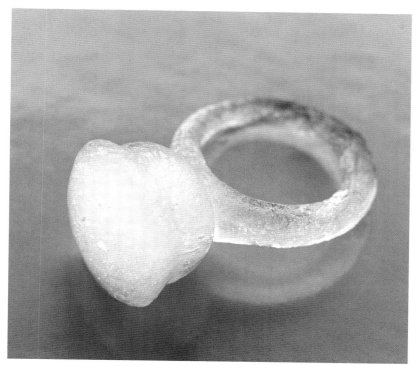

GLYNIS GARDNER

Love You Long Time | 2007

5 X 3.5 X 3 CM

Ice

PHOTO BY JAMES KIRK

I love this brooch for its simplicity. When I look at it, depending on my mood, it can be **funny, sad, and even slightly frightening**. There is a ghostly look about it. I think it would look lovely on or against a very white wall. ■ *Daphne Krinos*

Not many Künzli pieces represent an **emotion**. This one cries like Norwegian painter Edvard Munch's *The Scream*. ■ *Ruudt Peters*

OTTO KÜNZLI
Friend | 1997
7 CM IN DIAMETER
Brass; painted
PHOTO BY ARTIST

A clear, recognizable image, like in a **child's drawing**, pure in color and shape. It reminds me of a pictogram, but with a double layer that gives it a special expression. **You see what you want to see.** ■ *Karin Seufert*

PHOTO BY DEBORAH SMITH

This is the most **surprising idea**. It's funny, it's lovely, and it's spontaneously photographed without any finery! ■ *Birgit Laken*

So easy, so simple, no pretensions; **seized with emotion**.
■ *Miriam Verbeek*

Material has always been central to contemporary jewelry practices. The divisions of how material informs the idea, or how the idea has formed around the material, are both subtle nuances hinting at its communication. This image sums it all up: the material is **from the people, for the people**, and how convincing the transformation of that process can be! Fran's lei is worn with pride!
■ *Peter Deckers*

FRAN ALLISON
From "how to make a rabbit from a sock" to "how to make a necklace from a frock" | *2004–2005*
110 X 40 CM
Fabric, silver, steel cable, resin;
hand fabricated, sewed, constructed

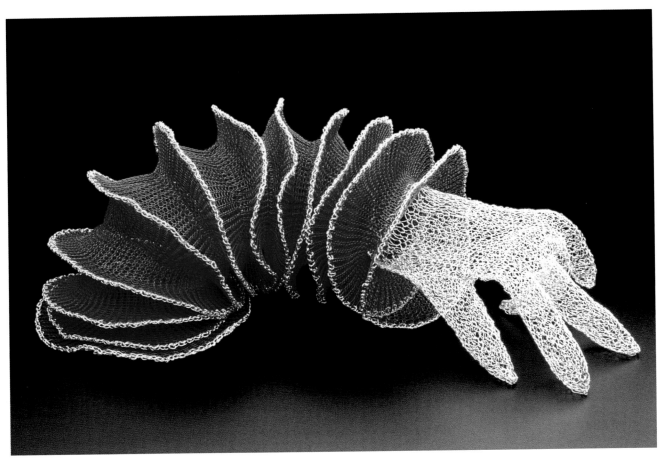

ARLINE FISCH
Bracelet and Glove | 1999

52 X 13 X 13 CM

Coated copper wire, fine silver; machine
knitted, hand knitted, crocheted

PHOTO BY WILLIAM GULLETTE
COLLECTION OF SMITHSONIAN ART MUSEUM'S
RENWICK GALLERY, WASHINGTON, DC

Stunning object with a sense of humor. ~ *Charlotte De Syllas*

KIRSTI REINSBORG GROV
Double Soapbubble—Blower | 2004
12 X 8 X 2.5 CM
Copper, 14-karat gold, enamel,
rubber band, soap water

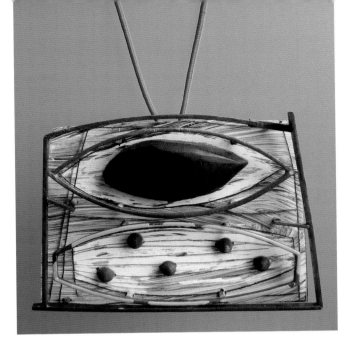

Within a framed structure
lies a playful interplay
of line, shape, and
color. Sometimes subtle,
sometimes bold, these
elements combine to
create a dance in
which each element is
exactly as it needs to be.

■ *Barbara Cohen*

RAMON PUIG CUYÀS
Tempora Si Fuerint Nibula
(from the series Imago Mundi, 1150) | 2007
5.5 X 6 X 1 CM
Silver, plastic, nickel silver, wood,
volcanic stones, acrylic paint; assembled
PHOTO BY ARTIST

This brooch is emblematic of all the things I love about
Ramon Puig Cuyàs' work—the harmony he achieves
with disparate materials; his compositions so beautifully
balanced, yet **unexpected** and his unabashed love
affair with color. His work makes the body a most intimate
and inviting gallery. ■ *Nisa Blackmon*

RAMON PUIG CUYÀS
Red Bird | 2002
6 X 5 X 1 CM
Silver, wood, plastic, quartz, paper, coral; assembled
PHOTO BY ARTIST

MONIKA BRUGGER
Sewn with Red Thread | 2007

34.4 X 31.2 X 3 CM

Cotton chemise, thimble, silver, silk thread,
gold needle, wood

PHOTO BY ARTIST

MARKIAN GALANDIUK
Corinthian | 2002
36 X 21.5 X 0.5 CM
Zippers
PHOTO BY ARTIST

I gasped when I first saw this piece! I love the use of a humble material in a way that embodies such **duality and opposition**. It is delicate, yet defiant; soft but appearing uncomfortable in the way that it stiffly references Corinthian columns and Elizabethan collars. I appreciate the subtle reference to carotid and jugular blood flow created by the opposing orientation of the zippers, and the vulnerability conferred by their action and location. ▪ *Nisa Blackmon*

This necklace is intriguing with its simplicity, delicacy, and elegance. **Transparency and light** play important roles. When single parts overlap, it looks like thin ice. Red beads make an unostentatious accent of the jewelry. ■ *Pavel Herynek*

SUJIN PARK
Folding II | 2007
34 X 16 X 2.8 CM
Plastic sheet, plastic
beads; scored, folded

PHOTO BY MYUNG UK HUH

NICOLE JACQUARD
Fragments I | 2008
2.5 X 7 X 7.5 CM
Plastic resin, fine silver, gypsum powder,
thermoplastic; rapid prototyped
PHOTO BY KEVIN MONTAGUE

It appeals to me when little stories are told in jewelry, or when you can make your own story. As Mirjam says herself, "my goal is to create little **characters that communicate** with viewers in nonverbal ways." You wonder what this pendant is. Some underwater creature maybe, with its own secrets? The use of white and blue colors gives the piece something **dreamy and vulnerable**. Techniques, such as folding the metal, give this jewel the appearance of a sketch, something **open and playful**.

— *Ingeborg Vandamme*

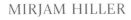

MIRJAM HILLER
Sucker | 2006
12 X 4.6 X 1.7 CM
Copper, enamel, rose quartz, thread; pressed, folded
PHOTOS BY JSOLDE GOLDERER

These **whimsical** rings evoke **fond memories** of the picnics my family took back in the 1960s and 1970s and the colorful melamine dishes we used. I can almost taste the potato salad! ■ *Ann L. Lumsden*

KAREN FLY
MelaMine Rings | 2007
EACH, 5 X 4 X 4 CM
Melamine; cut, carved
PHOTO BY STUART MCINTYRE

This pendant is asking for my attention all the time! Apart from its **perfect aesthetic shape**, this pendant keeps **intriguing** me.

■ *Birgit Laken*

This defines the word "pendant" perfectly for me. Beautiful **proportions**, perfect choice of **materials**, and it would look amazing worn on simple, monochrome clothing. I think it would make me feel very **balanced** if I could look at it every day!

■ *Daphne Krinos*

CASTELLO HANSEN
Pendant | 2002
12 X 6 X 3 CM
Cibatool, paint, silver, string; oxidized
PHOTO BY LARS GUNDERSEN

BEVERLEY PRICE
*Neckpiece for the Emperor's Gold
Clothing Circa 2006* | 2005
43 X 20 X 5 CM
Plastic, brass; laminated
PHOTO BY ARTIST

The beauty of this brooch is the rich pattern, texture, and the choice of soft neutral colors. The interlocking plastic units remind me of an ice crystal. I am intrigued by the construction of the brooch and the way the colors contrast to create depth and three dimensions. I imagine it to be light and delicate, and yet it is made from a robust material. ▪ *Julie Blyfield*

SVENJA JOHN
Ice | 2003
7 X 10.8 X 8.6 CM
Stainless steel, polycarbonate
PHOTO BY KEVIN SPRAGUE

This piece looks like a ring that would be used to **shackle** a prisoner to the wall. Simple, elegant, and strong. **Are we held prisoner by our own lust for more?**

■ *Mia Maljojoki*

OTTO KÜNZLI
Gold Makes Blind | 1980
GOLD SPHERE, 1.2 CM IN DIAMETER
Rubber, gold
PHOTO BY ARTIST

JIRO KAMATA
Sunny Pendant | 2005
7.5 X 7.5 X 1.5 CM
Plastic lenses, silver; laser carved
PHOTO BY ARTIST

Uli's work of screen-printed images on silicone rubber makes a very clever statement about the preciousness of jewelry. The work adorns but doesn't weigh us down, physically or psychologically. ▪ *Susan Kasson Sloan*

ULI

Diamonds and Pearls | 2006

34 X 20 X 0.5 CM
Silicone rubber, textile;
screen printed
PHOTO BY ARTIST

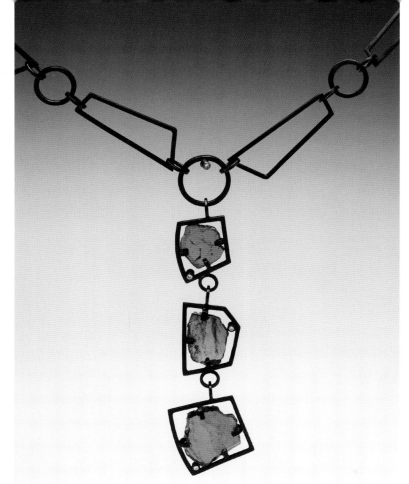

Krinos's *Necklace* combines all the factors that I incorporate when I design pieces. The use of the unusual stone, its **minimal containment**, off-setting the oxidized sterling silver, the color, and the open shapes that give **balance** and **weight** to an otherwise **visually airy** piece—her whole approach appeals to me!

■ *Janis Kerman*

DAPHNE KRINOS
Necklace | 2007
11 X 0.4 CM; 47 CM LONG
Silver, tourmalines, diamonds; oxidized
PHOTO BY JOËL DEGEN

SUSAN KASSON SLOAN
Resin Brooch I | 2005
14 X 4.4 CM
Epoxy resin, pigment,
sterling silver
PHOTO BY RALPH GABRINER

What I like in this work is that I go into **another world**;
a space of aliens where I do not belong. ▪ *Ruudt Peters*

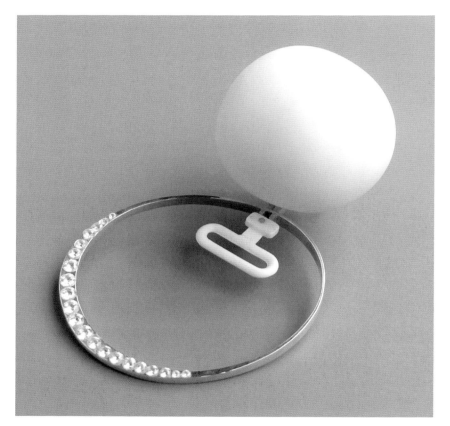

JANTJE FLEISCHHUT
Die Weissen Berge Series: Luminary | 2007
4 X 8.5 X 5 CM
Epoxy, fiberglass, zirconia, silver
PHOTO BY ARTIST

Sensual image and subject. Asymmetrical earrings add an unexpected surprise to this **provocative** interpretation of what is possible in an earring format. ■ *Tom Muir*

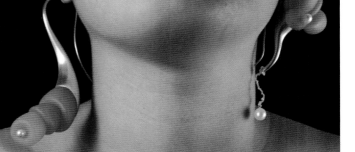

MASAKO ONODERA

The Mating Season | 2006

9.5 X 4.5 X 4 CM AND 11.5 X 2.6 X 6 CM

Sterling silver, freshwater pearls, polyethylene cord, rubber; formed, fabricated, dyed

PHOTOS BY ARTIST

This looks like some kind of **underwater creature**, but is made from materials used to build houses. What kind of sound does it make when you put it on? ▪ *Mia Maljojoki*

CAROL-LYNN SWOL
Book Bracelet | 2003
11.4 X 11.4 X 7.6 CM
Tyvek, dye, thread; machine sewn
PHOTO BY KEVIN MONTAGUE AND MICHAEL CAVANAGH

The piece Karin created translates **a quiet interlacing of thought** through the subtle use of shape and gesture.

■ *Nicole Jacquard*

KARIN SEUFERT
Untitled | 2007
9 X 6 X 4 CM
PVC, reconstructed coral,
thread, elastic, steel;
sewed, glued, cut
PHOTO BY ARTIST

The **fantasy** form, lively color, and refined surface are present in all of Peter Chang's bracelets, but this is my favorite because of its whimsy and **animation**. It would be such fun to wear. ■ *Arline M. Fisch*

Complex work two and three dimensionally. **Dramatic** form and image. **Innovative** use of materials and approach to the bracelet format. Emotionally, this is a fun and **exuberant** work. ■ *Tom Muir*

Futuristically whimsical, as if you've landed in the world of Alice in Wonderland in 2050. A pleasure to behold, making my inner child smile. ■ *emiko oye*

Truly **inspirational design and craftsmanship**. Peter Chang's ability to take plastic as a material to a new level is to be admired. ■ *Kathryn Wardill*

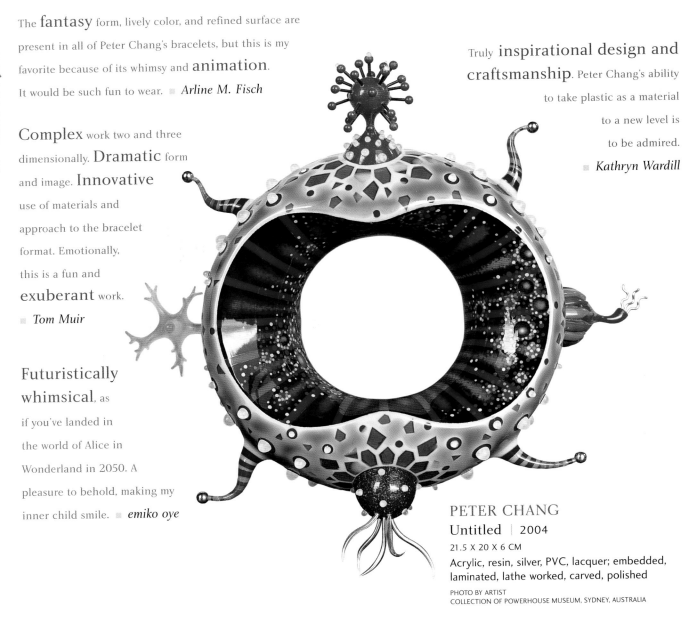

PETER CHANG
Untitled | 2004

21.5 X 20 X 6 CM

Acrylic, resin, silver, PVC, lacquer; embedded, laminated, lathe worked, carved, polished

PHOTO BY ARTIST
COLLECTION OF POWERHOUSE MUSEUM, SYDNEY, AUSTRALIA

Shay's pieces make me smile. His combination of color, shape, and distinct style says, "Notice me!" His pieces call out to be held and admired, and of course, worn! All three pieces I have chosen express his unique ability to **master color and assembly** to create very unique oeuvres. One can immediately recognize his work, but each piece is **unique** in style and composition.

■ *Janis Kerman*

SHAY LAHOVER
Untitled | 2007
2.5 X 1.9 X 1.9 CM
18-karat gold, 24-karat gold,
uncut ruby, drusy, rubies, diamonds
PHOTO BY R. H. HENSLEIGH

JANTJE FLEISCHHUT

Sateliten 2 Series | 2003

LARGEST, 4 X 5 X 9 CM

Found plastic, epoxy,
fiberglass, silver, pearls,
found rubber, citrine

PHOTOS BY ARTIST

The pig is one of the most **humorous** pieces of jewelry I ever have seen. It closed and opened the eyes with the big ears. ■ *Ruudt Peters*

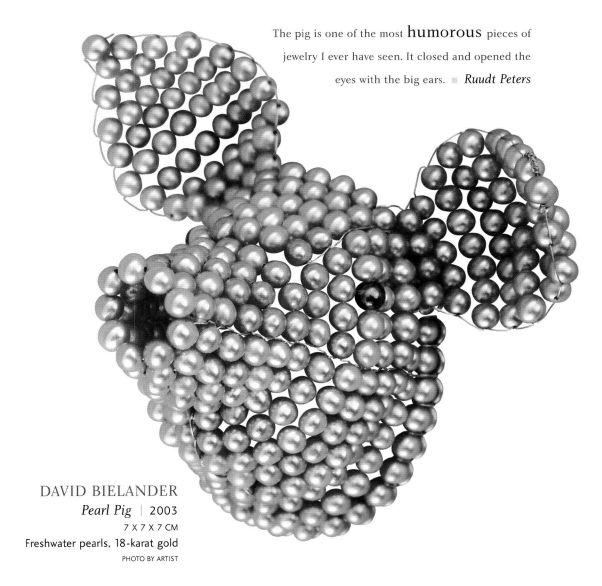

DAVID BIELANDER
Pearl Pig | 2003
7 X 7 X 7 CM
Freshwater pearls, 18-karat gold
PHOTO BY ARTIST

Because of its **expressive** appearance and the artist's wit and humor, this brooch is not easy to overlook. Its childlike playfulness and ease, rare qualities today, make this piece so **charming**.

■ *Pavel Herynek*

FELIEKE VAN DER LEEST
Tree Frog with Knickerbockers | 2003
11.5 X 8 X 3 CM
Textile, rubber, gold, store-bought toy;
crocheted, forged
PHOTO BY EDDO HARTMANN

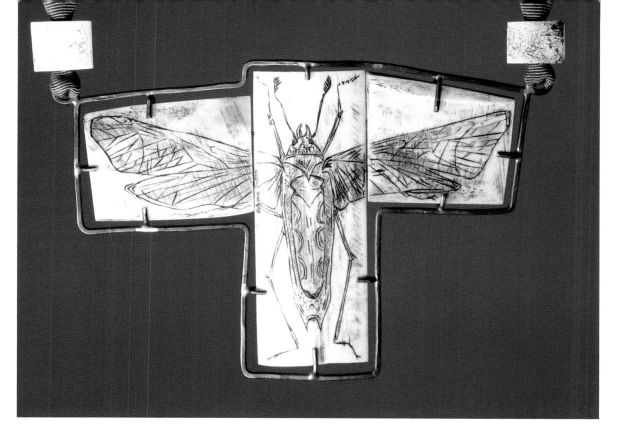

THOMAS HILL
Bug Pendant | 2004
11.4 X 10.2 CM
Bone, ink, brass, silk; engraved
PHOTOS BY MIKE HOLMES

Going against the grain of how jewelry typically works, like a dog embellishing and guarding the owner, Ted takes our hand and quietly whispers through this piece that it is time to drop our **vanity** and allow ourselves to **be humble** while others shine. ■ *Natalya Pinchuk*

A combination of the **grotesque**, the **funny**, and the **profane**. The humorous narrative is direct while being informed by jewelry history yet remaining thoroughly modern.

■ *Lisa and Scott Cylinder*

ATELIER TED NOTEN
Turbo Princess | 1995
7.5 X 15 X 2.5 CM
Mouse with pearl necklace, acrylic, silver, steel wire; cast, whitened
PHOTO BY ARTIST

All the **sublime** qualities of abstraction, minimal form, subtle surface coloration, and no obvious messages to ponder are in this piece. And, as if that is not enough, this piece also manages to put a **smile** on your face.

■ *Talya Baharal*

POLY NIKOLOPOULOU
Saligari | 2007
6 X 10 X 1 CM
Sterling silver; hammered, oxidized
PHOTO BY ARTIST

To present body parts inside a glass bubble made me cry. It's **SO** **fragile** in all ways.

▪ *Ruudt Peters*

NANNA MELLAND
Fragment of Life II | 2003
6 X 3.5 X 3.5 CM
Plastic, sterling silver, glass;
cast, hand blown
PHOTOS BY ARTIST

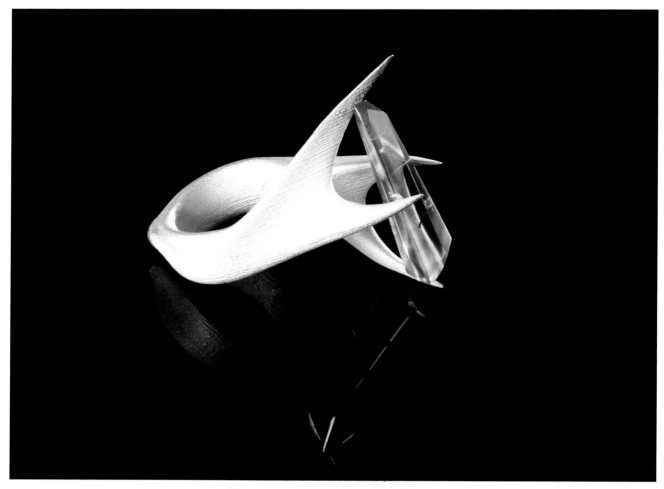

HAGEN GAMISCH
Aedes Sapientia | 2006
5 X 4.6 X 3 CM
Silver, aquamarine; CAD, sandcast, cut
PHOTO BY PETRA JASCHKE

LESLIE MATTHEWS
Untitled | 2005
LARGEST, 7 X 4 X 3 CM
Sterling silver, silk
cord; oxidized
PHOTO BY GRANT HANCOCK

Such **delicate** pieces of
paper-like forms that
seem so fragile, as though
they have been lifted directly
from a sketchbook page.

Sim Luttin

JAN WEHRENS
Brooch | 2001
7.4 X 10.5 X 4.4 CM
Silver, patina
PHOTO BY ARTIST

Wonderful, lively imagery with great technique forms a fully realized piece from a new maker. ■ *Thomas Hill*

ALLYSON BONE
Fur Eisen | 2007
PENDANT, 3.5 X 10.5 X 1.3 CM
Sterling silver, liver of sulfur; etched, hydraulic pressed, cast, soldered
PHOTOS BY ARTIST

These beautiful hollow silver rings project **strength and boldness,** contrasting with **delicacy and lightness**. The textured pierced holes create a rich overall surface pattern. There is a **strong relationship** between the three rings in their form and proportions. ▪ *Julie Blyfield*

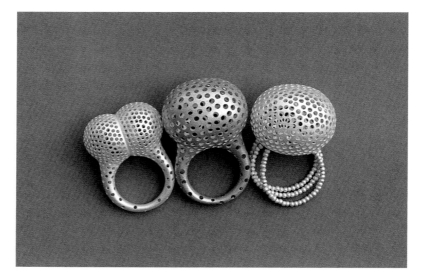

MASCHA MOJE
3 Rings | 2000
LARGEST, 3 X 2 X 1.5 CM
Silver; hollow constructed, raised, soldered, drilled
PHOTO BY ARTIST

KARIN SEUFERT
Untitled | 2005
30 X 11.5 X 2.5 CM
PVC, thread; punched,
sewed, glued
PHOTO BY ARTIST

This pendant is an **intricate** and **sensitive** formal study of repetition and contrast. ■ *Jessica Calderwood*

JACQUELINE RYAN
Untitled | 1999
PENDANT, 8 X 4.2 X 4.2 CM
18-karat gold, enamel;
hand fabricated
PHOTO BY ARTIST

Although evident as jewelry, the work is **autonomous** in character.

This exemplifies how you can use tradition to create something

never before seen. Beautiful. ■ *Ralph Bakker*

JACQUELINE RYAN
Untitled | 2000
EACH, 2.8 X 2.2 X 1.4 CM
18-karat palladium white gold;
hand fabricated
PHOTO BY GIOVANNI CORVAJA

Sim's piece **captures a moment** in time—
the point at which you are just about to make a wish.

■ *Nicole Jacquard*

SIM LUTTIN
Just Dandy | 2007
7 CM IN DIAMETER
Sterling silver; hand
fabricated, threaded
PHOTO BY KEVIN MONTAGUE

This collar is made so beautifully. I love the **sawing** work. The finishing…everything is **perfect**. Lovely! ■ *Francis Willemstijn*

VELETA VANCZA

Neck Lace/Neck Brace | 2000

11.4 X 17.8 X 17.8 CM

Sterling silver, pearls; hand pierced, formed, fabricated

PHOTO BY BOB BARRETT

SUZANNE AMENDOLARA

Untitled II | 2006

EACH, 2 X 2 CM

14-karat gold, diamond; cast

PHOTO BY ARTIST
COLLECTION OF KAREN ERNST AND ERIC CALDWELL

TOM FERRERO
Collar of the Chancellor | 2007
43 X 43 X 0.6 CM
Sterling silver, steel; cast, fabricated, riveted
PHOTOS BY KEVIN MONTAGUE

A **graceful** composition of **flowing** curves that divide and recombine. The twined structure in high-karat gold gives a rich and subtle texture over the entire necklace. ■ *Arline M. Fisch*

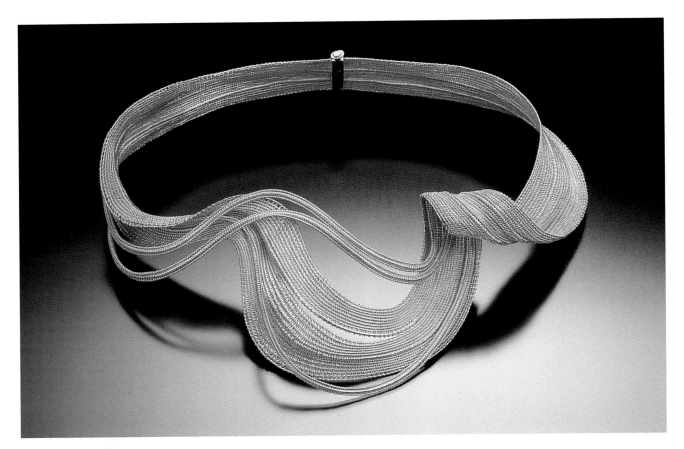

MARY LEE HU
Choker #88 | 2005

24.5 X 24 X 4.5 CM

18-karat gold, 22-karat gold; twined, fabricated

PHOTO BY DOUG YAPLE
PRIVATE COLLECTION

This ring is a rare example of technical research successfully applied to contemporary jewelry. You do not often find jewelry designers with a scientific method who are **committed to technical research**. Giovanni Corvaja is surely one of them. ■ *Stefano Marchetti*

GIOVANNI CORVAJA
Untitled | 2000
2.2 X 1.2 X 2.2 CM
Fine wire; assembled
PHOTO BY ARTIST

This piece shows the incredible **sensitivity** of the artist. ■ *Tom Munsteiner*

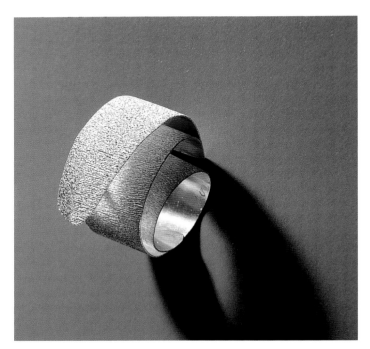

ANNAMARIA ZANELLA
Untitled | 1998
3 X 2 CM
Gold
PHOTO BY LORENZO TRENTO

A wonderful combination of incredibly **refined technique** with a clear understanding of **form and space**. The historical reference is a rare honor to the rich Italian goldsmithing tradition.

■ *Charon Kransen*

STEFANO MARCHETTI
Brooch | 2001
5 X 5 X 5 CM
22-karat red gold, 14-karat yellow gold
PHOTO BY ROBERTO SORDI

I like how Christine let the **dramatic** look of the agate **speak for itself,** yet designed the piece with the extra enhancement of the Mexican opal and copper-like metal. ◼ *Gurhan Orhan*

CHRISTINE HAFERMALZ-WHEELER
Agate and Opal Necklace | 2008
5.5 X 6.5 X 0.5 CM
Agate, Mexican opal, 18-karat gold, shibori
AGATE CARVED BY DIETER LORENZ
PHOTO BY DAVID WHEELER

I like the way the soft forms and colors of the gold
elements that surround the amber **mimic**
the platelets within the stone and create
the **illusion** of liquid depth. It's
like a great October day with all its
fall colors. ■ *George Sawyer*

BARBARA HEINRICH
Amber Brooch | 2003
8 X 5 CM
18-karat gold, Baltic amber;
hand fabricated, roller printed
PHOTO BY TIM CALLAHAN

Eleanor's piece appears to exist on **multiple planes of light**. It
projects so much **implied motion** that I can intuit what it looked
like a moment ago and visualize its future form. ■ *Jeff & Susan Wise*

ELEANOR MOTY
Autumnal Veil Brooch | 2008
7.2 X 4.3 X 1.2 CM
Sterling silver, 22-karat gold, 18-karat
gold, quartz, iron oxide, citrines
QUARTZ BY HERMAN PETRY; CITRINES BY TOM MUNSTEINER
PHOTO BY ARTIST

MARIANNE HUNTER

The Universe Dances | 2008

5.4 X 27.3 X 1 CM

Enamel, quartz with pyrite, diamonds, pallasite,
rutile, fossil coral, hessonite garnet, 24-karat gold,
14-karat gold, 18-karat gold; fabricated, engraved

PHOTO BY HAP SAKWA

This necklace is all about **abundance**—an abundance of gems, colors, textures, techniques, sizes, and shapes. It's the collagist's approach to the materials that I most appreciate. Your eye first sees the overall design, and then you focus in and start to notice the variety of stones and the colors of the enamels. A shade of orange enamel on one side is picked up by a complementary shade of a gemstone on the other. It all **resonates and sings** together like an orchestra. ■ *Cindy Edelstein*

THOMAS HERMAN

Indonesian Plume Agate Brooch | 2008

4.3 X 4.3 X 0.8 CM

18-karat gold, Indonesian plume agate, diamonds;
turned, cast, chased, engraved, saw pierced

PHOTO BY ALLEN BRYAN

In these beautiful earrings, Barbara Heinrich combines nature's hardest material, diamond, with delicate leaf forms rendered in 18-karat gold. I see the diamonds as **tiny droplets of water glistening** on the leaves. The overall effect is stunning, and the technical mastery impressive! ■ *Ann L. Lumsden*

Barbara takes a nature-inspired motif often used in jewelry, but adds an **unexpected twist** with her use of both brilliant diamonds and diamond briolettes.

■ *Gurhan Orhan*

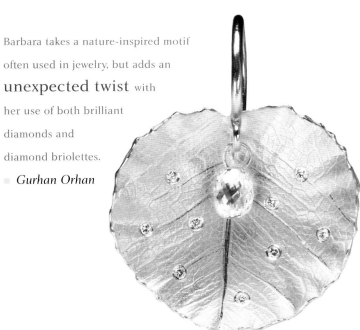

BARBARA HEINRICH
Lotus Leaf Earrings | 2008
EACH, 2.8 X 2.1 X 1 CM
18-karat yellow gold, diamond briolette drops, diamonds; hand fabricated, chased, surface set
PHOTO BY TIM CALLAHAN

TERRI LOGAN
Slate & Rock Series | 2003
EACH, 2.5 X 2.5 X 1.3 CM
Sterling silver, slate, rock, concrete, patina; constructed, cast, inlaid
PHOTO BY JERRY ANTHONY

Tami's work has been a big influence on me since my undergraduate days. Her **asymmetric symmetry** is so engaging and fun. ■ *Nanz Aalund*

TAMI DEAN
Quirky Girls | 1998
EACH, 4.5 X 1.8 X 2.8 CM
14-karat palladium white gold, 18-karat gold, opals, diamonds; hand forged, fabricated
PHOTO BY HAP SAKWA

In *Segment Break II*, the forms are smooth and organic, and the thin **translucent** acrylic gives the necklace a look of **weightlessness.** ▪ *Linda MacNeil*

BETTY HEALD

Segment Break II | 1997

27 X 26.5 X 1 CM

Acrylic, sterling silver, stainless steel, rubber; heat formed, fabricated, chemically dyed

PHOTO BY NORMAN WATKINS

LEE RAMSEY HAGA

Japanese Shields | 2001

EACH, 2.7 X 2.2 X 0.3 CM

Shibuishi, 18-karat gold, patina;
reticulated, hand fabricated

PHOTO BY HAP SAKWA

I am pulled toward Jan Smith's work for a number of reasons—the treatment of surfaces, the **mark making**, and the combination of textures and materials. I enjoy the way she approaches the enamel. This approach results in a wonderful use of color and adds a deeper **dimension** to the work. *Donna D'Aquino*

JAN SMITH
Blue Rectangle within Circle | 2002
4.1 X 0.6 CM
Enamel, copper, sterling silver, 22-karat
gold bimetal; champlevé, sgraffito
PHOTO BY DOUG YAPLE

Kathryn has **given life** to a synthetic material, sharing a new species and vocabulary. As buds emerge, her pieces question the artificial nature associated with the materials. ■ *Nicole Jacquard*

Kathryn Wardill's *White Pod Series* is an **elegant exploration** of form and material. ■ *Donna D'Aquino*

KATHRYN WARDILL
White Pod Series (Bracelet, Brooch, and Three Rings) | 2007
BRACELET, 12 X 8 X 3 CM;
BROOCH, 8 X 3 X 2 CM;
EACH RING, 3 X 3 X 1.5 CM
Plastic, silver, steel; hand carved
PHOTOS BY ARTIST

The marble exterior is coarse, cold, and cloudy. The gold interior is smooth, warm, and reflective. Jim Cotter's *Rock Ring* uses **extreme contrast** exceptionally well to **intensify** the effect of both materials. ■ *Marthe Le Van*

JIM COTTER
Rock Ring | 2000
3.8 X 3 X 1.6 CM
Marble, 14-karat yellow gold
PHOTO BY R. HEDSTROM

Rings with balls and branches—the power is the

imagination. ■ *Ruudt Peters*

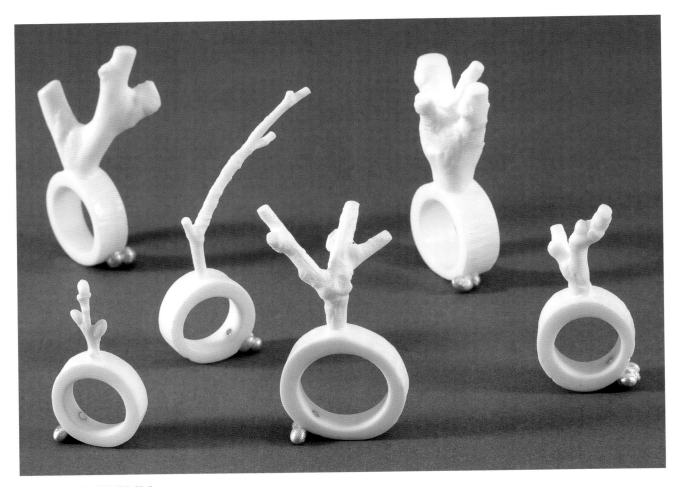

SUSANNE KLEMM
Mutation Rings | 2007
VARIOUS DIMENSIONS
Sterling silver, epoxy
resin; cast
PHOTO BY HAROLD STRAK

  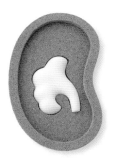  

The pendants themselves evoke such beauty and craftsmanship, and then conceptually the piece is so complete. The photograph expresses everything so **seamlessly**. It is very **satisfying** to take in the image on the page. It is one of those pieces that **lingers on** in the mind to ponder after the book is closed. ■ *Deborah Lozier*

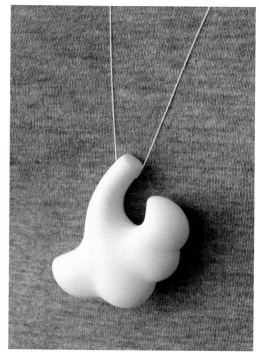

LEONOR HIPÓLITO
Transplant | 2007
VARIOUS DIMENSIONS
Cork, polyester
PHOTOS BY ARTIST

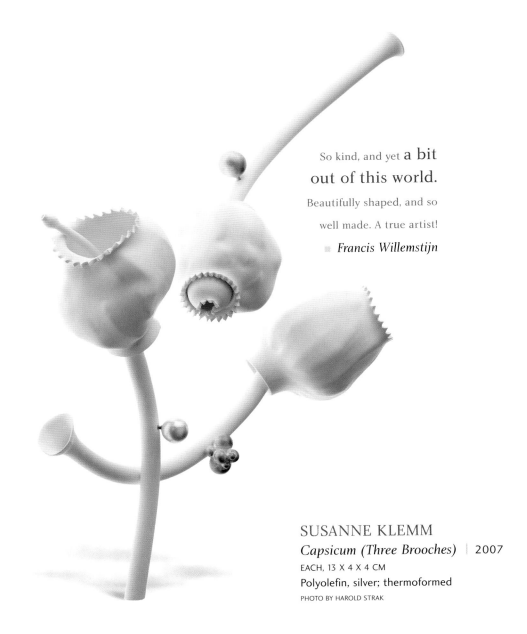

So kind, and yet **a bit out of this world.**

Beautifully shaped, and so well made. A true artist!

■ *Francis Willemstijn*

SUSANNE KLEMM
Capsicum (Three Brooches) | 2007
EACH, 13 X 4 X 4 CM
Polyolefin, silver; thermoformed
PHOTO BY HAROLD STRAK

There's a **beautiful silence** with this work. It's delicate, original in the way the material is handled, and the shapes and materials are brought together. I love the **non-logic** of the work and find it altogether very poetic and strong. ▪ *Katja Prins*

These pieces are so **delicate and quiet**, relating to each other so well, yet still strong on their own. I really respond to how she seems to be **drawing in space**, creating beautiful lines and volume.

▪ *Deborah Lozier*

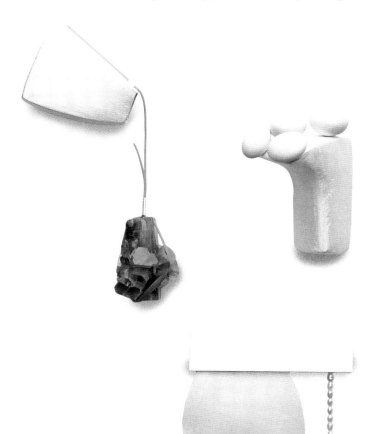

IRIS BODEMER
Untitled | 1999
LARGEST, 11 X 6 X 2 CM
Silver, aragonite, plastic, pebbles, pearls
PHOTOS BY JULIAN KIRSCHLER

This is a **frisky** ring. Its **animated** spirit and **eccentric** form make this flirtatious little creature **irresistible**. ■ *Marthe Le Van*

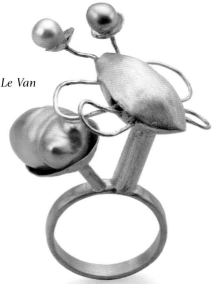

MARIA PACE PELLEGRINI
Pupa | 2003
4 X 2.8 X 2.4 CM
18-karat gold, Tahitian
pearls; constructed
PHOTO BY FEDERICO CAVICCHIOLI

The **mysterious, yet strangely familiar,** shapes and the sensual quality of the white enamel surface intrigue me. Her use of black outlines, playful connecting tabs reminiscent of cutout doll clothing, and the juxtaposition of materials add to the delightful quirkiness of this pendant. ■ *Barbara Cohen*

The form of this pendant presents small openings that invite the viewer to **seek refuge** inside its hollow space. At the same time, the openings **project outward like mouths** making sound. I appreciate the play between *Sucker's* quiet white introspection and its quirky, humorous reaching out. ■ *Cappy Counard*

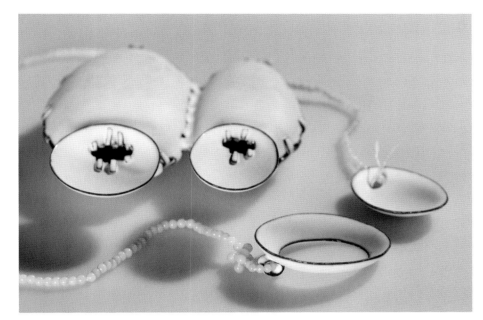

MIRJAM HILLER
Sucker | 2006

10 X 7 X 2 CM

Copper, enamel, coral, thread; pressed, folded

PHOTOS BY ISOLDE GOLDERER

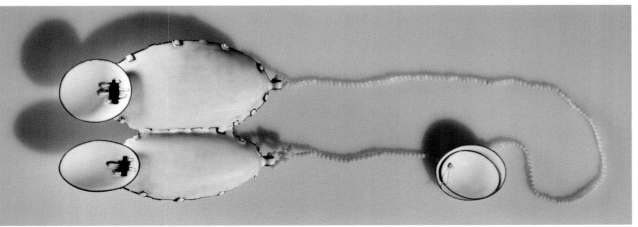

Some of the jewelry I have appreciated most over the last few years is by Beate Klockmann, in particular this ring. It is one of the first pieces I had the pleasure of seeing. The **dissonant movement** of the metal is perhaps one of the most successful examples of this treatment, recalling the **art of origami**.

■ *Stefano Marchetti*

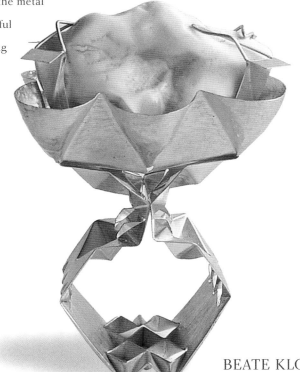

BEATE KLOCKMANN
Big Amber Ring | 2002
7 X 4.5 X 3 CM
Amber, 18-karat gold; hammered, milled, folded, soldered
PHOTO BY ARTIST

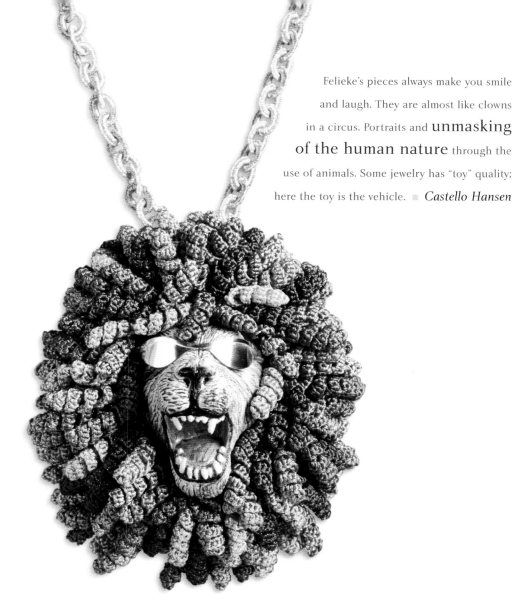

Felieke's pieces always make you smile and laugh. They are almost like clowns in a circus. Portraits and **unmasking of the human nature** through the use of animals. Some jewelry has "toy" quality; here the toy is the vehicle. ■ *Castello Hansen*

FELIEKE VAN DER LEEST

Brian the Lion | 2003

15 X 12 X 5 CM

Textile, plastic animal, gold;
crocheted, hand fabricated

PHOTO BY EDDO HARTMANN

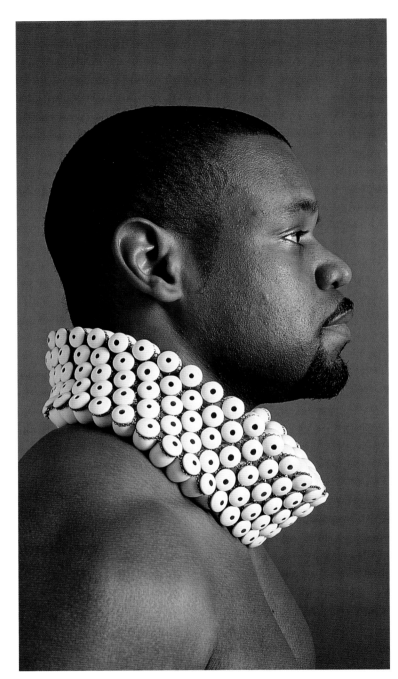

A sequential distribution of many identical elements gives this piece a **natural form**. I like the contrast between the use of a very **fragile** material and the **strong** visual impact.

Barbara Paganin

PETER HOOGEBOOM
Spanish Collar | 1995
7 X 63 X 2 CM
Ceramic, silver
PHOTO BY HENNI VAN BEEK

An open vessel of twisted, overlapping planes draws the viewer into the *Collector's Ring* by Ingjerd Hanevold. Intriguing because of its scale, its function, and its title, this dramatic, generously sized ring stands tall on the wearer's finger. The lidded container is actually useable as a vessel to hold small items, a feature that connects it to historical rings that held stones, potions, and even poison. The double meaning of the title refers to the fact that it is a container into which one can put a small collection of items, and it is also an object for jewelry collectors to contemplate purchasing. ▪ *Marjorie K. Schick*

INGJERD HANEVOLD
Collector's Ring | 2001
6 X 4.5 CM
Oxidized silver, seeds, cork
PHOTO BY ARTIST

BARBARA PAGANIN

Epicarpo | 1998

LEFT, 2.7 X 1.4 CM

Fine gold, 18-karat gold, oxidized
sterling silver, freshwater pearls

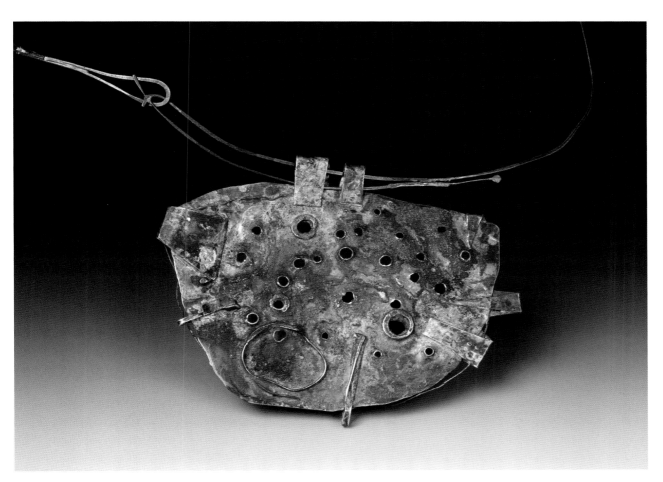

TALYA BAHARAL
Urban Landscape #33 | 2006
8 X 10.8 X 0.3 CM
Sterling silver, iron, steel,
copper, gold; fabricated
PHOTO BY GENE GNIDA

The composition of the brooch breaks reality into a **fragmented** and poetic view of a **deconstructed cityscape**. The organic back adds to an urban object. This poetic brooch is subtle, but **powerful** in its perceptual reading. ■ *Peter Deckers*

REBECCA HANNON
Rooftops Brooch | 2003
5.1 X 6.4 X 0.6 CM
Silver, gold, photograph; soldered, cut, reassembled
PHOTOS BY ARTIST

How do you join flat pieces together and make them one? Will it only be one when the **signs of joining** are eliminated, or do you find beauty in the evidence of the connection process? Seams never looked more **intentional** or more **beautiful** to me. ■ *Talya Baharal*

ALESSIA SEMERARO
Jazz Band #2 | 2002
4.5 X 8 X 1 CM
Iron, silver; pierced, soldered, riveted
PHOTO BY RAYBOOM

This is somehow just right. ■ *Melanie Bilenker*

BIRGIT LAKEN
Big Thumbnail | 2006
2.8 X 7.5 X 2.6 CM
Phenol resin fabric; shaped
PHOTO BY ARTIST

A stunning and beautiful piece of art. The dark alpaca with the red sealing wax, as if it is about to be poured out. One of my favorite pieces of all time. ■ *Francis Willemstijn*

KATJA PRINS
Untitled | 2003
10 X 12 X 8 CM
Alpaca, sealing wax
PHOTO BY EDDO HARTMANN

Is there anything more **unexpected** than this set of rings, yet so eternal in its message? From the playfulness and excitement of **attraction** to the point when there is no longer any power for **ignition**, a love story is executed superbly and in innovative fashion.

■ *Nina Basharova*

JULIA MARIA KÜNNAP
Light My Fire | 2004

LARGE, 2.5 X 2.5 X 0.7 CM;
SMALL, 2.2 X 2.2 X 0.3 CM

18-karat white gold, LED, battery, Herkon switch, magnet

PHOTOS BY ARTIST
PRIVATE COLLECTION

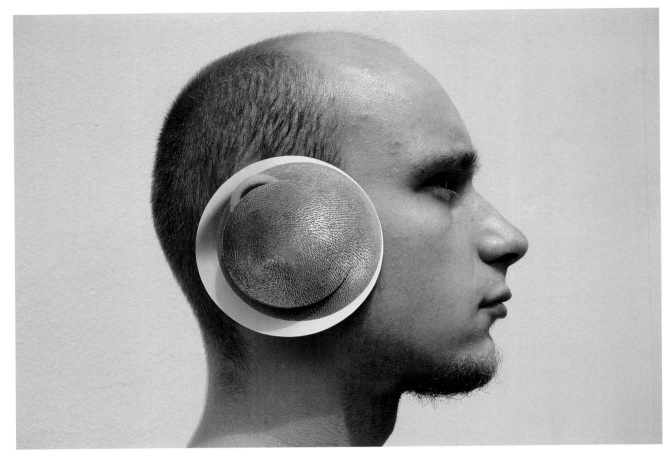

PAVEL HERYNEK

Ear Ornament | 2002
*(from the Ear Ornaments
series, 2002–2006)*

10 CM IN DIAMETER
Cardboard, postcard; cut
PHOTO BY ARTIST

Pavel Herynek is a savvy designer. This earring, cut from a printed postcard, is dynamite. The large scale of it works well on the head, and the printed spiraling effect makes it appear as if it is referring to sound waves or short hair growing out of a central point. Both of these interpretations connect the image on the postcard to either an ear or a head. I am drawn to the fact that the form appears as if it is convex, but because it is a postcard, this may be an optical illusion. I find it exciting to imagine this as being either flat or three-dimensional. The perfection of the design of the earring illustrates that it was carefully considered, yet I like that the actual execution of it was probably very short in terms of time. ■ *Marjorie K. Schick*

GERD ROTHMANN
Fingerprint Wedding Rings | 2004
EACH, 0.8 X 2.1 X 2.2 CM
18-karat white gold; cast, fabricated
PHOTO BY STEFAN FRIEDEMANN

This necklace has a beautiful, **ethereal** quality that is heightened by the dream-like feeling captured in the photograph. ▪ *Sue Amendolara*

JIANG MEI-FANG
A Trip for Packing | 2005
18 X 18 X 300 CM
Brass wire, coated copper wire
PHOTO BY KUEN LUNG TSAI

MARY HALLAM PEARSE

Feeding Desire | 2008

8.9 X 6.4 X 1 CM

Sterling silver, aluminum, pearls, glass

PHOTO BY ARTIST

This brooch espouses **commitment**. The moving wearer will precipitate a **ritual** based on the tactility of the paper corolla brushing on the face, the wearer's kinesthetic adjustments, and the shifting equilibrium and rhythm achieved. ▪ *Beverley Price*

Lightness, movement, delicacy, and the result is a **sumptuous** piece of beauty. ▪ *Claude Schmitz*

KAYO SAITO
Floating Brooch | 2001
10 TO 12 X 10 CM IN DIAMETER
Paper, polyester fiber, magnets
PHOTO BY ARTIST

Brilliant use of traditional mourning-jewelry materials in a fresh, contemporary concept. Wonderfully **quiet and contemplative** work. ▪ *Chris Irick*

For me, Melanie is one of the best artists in the United States because she transforms **narrative storytelling** through a modern-day visualization. Her drawings and use of hair are touching to me. ▪ *Ruudt Peters*

MELANIE BILENKER

Likeness | 2003

3.5 X 2.8 X 1 CM

Hair, epoxy resin, ivory piano key
laminate, sterling silver, ebony

PHOTO BY KEN YANOVIAK

The use of print under plastic forms a kind of **"story-as-jewel"** and creates a fascinating piece of graphic jewelry. ▪ *Andrea Wagner*

JANTJE FLEISCHHUT

Bubble | 2007

9 X 6.5 CM

14-karat gold, epoxy, print on foil

PHOTO BY ARTIST

I adore the humor in Felieke's work.

How could you have a bad day wearing this necklace?

■ *Chris Irick*

FELIEKE VAN DER LEEST
Gusz Goosz | 2006
12.5 X 4.5 X 4.5 CM
Textile, glass, plastic animal, gold,
topaz; crocheted, hand fabricated
PHOTO BY EDDO HARTMANN

Through the lightweight construction of these **iconic earrings,** Rachelle was able to circumvent the tedious restrictions present in making earrings. She **elevated the decorative to the sculptural.**

— *Seth Papac*

RACHELLE THIEWES
Shimmer | 2004
EACH, 13.6 X 3.6 X 3.6 CM
18-karat palladium white gold, silver
PHOTO BY ARTIST

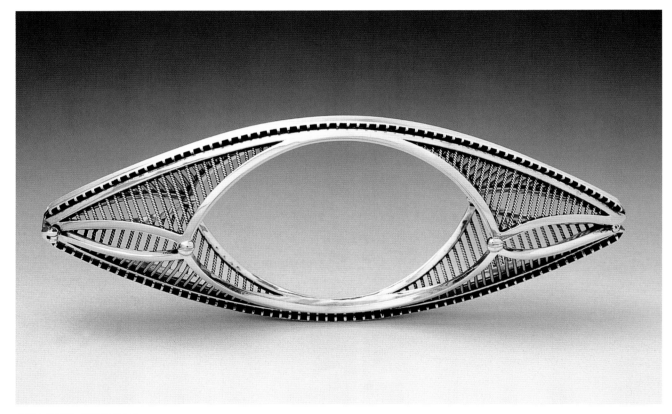

SERGEY JIVETIN

Bridge Bracelet | 1999

6 X 12 X 2 CM

Sterling silver; hand fabricated

PHOTO BY ARTIST
COLLECTION OF LISA M. BERMAN

It is difficult to define this structure as a ring, **audaciously extending in space** like an architectural item and totally **limiting the functionality of hands**. It may be seen as an extension-prosthesis of the body for a dancer or a body performer, or as a sculpture to be laid on a flat surface.

■ *Fabrizio Tridenti*

JEANNE BEAVER
The Space That Tension Occupies | 1998
5 X 33 X 1.3 CM
Sterling silver, stainless steel;
cold connected, soldered, hollow constructed
PHOTOS BY ARTIST

ADDAM
Venus Fly Wrap | 2004
12.4 X 12.4 X 9.4 CM
Sterling silver;
hand fabricated, soldered
PHOTO BY VICTOR FRANCE

ANTON CEPKA

Untitled | 1988

36 X 12.5 X 0.8 CM

Silver; cut, soldered

PHOTO BY ARTIST
PRIVATE COLLECTION

I like the **unconventional material** in this technique, not a straightforward solution. ■ *Ruudt Peters*

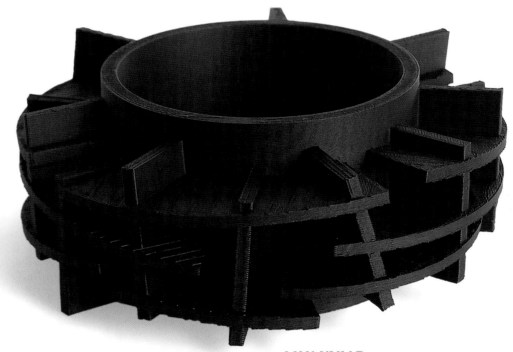

LILY YUNG
Planes Bracelet | 2007
11.4 X 11.4 X 5 CM
ABS plastic; rapid prototyped
PHOTO BY ARTIST

Lawrence Woodford's *Blossoms, Tree Stumps, and Marrow Pendants* are gorgeous in their simplicity. Referencing natural phenomena, they invite the wearer to enter their **dreamlike whorls**. Inside these **objects of contemplation**, one considers his place in life's cycle and mortality. ■ *Rebecca Hannon*

LAWRENCE WOODFORD

Blossoms, Tree Stumps, and
Marrow Pendants | 2007
LARGEST, 4.5 X 2 X 1.5 CM
Silver; constructed, deconstructed
PHOTO BY PAUL FOURNIER

What's intriguing about this piece is that it's quite **futuristic** in design, yet the feel of it is also quite **organic**.

■ *Gurhan Orhan*

NINA BASHAROVA
Milky Way & Black Hole | 2004
6 X 8 X 6 CM
Sterling silver; fabricated, cast, soldered
PHOTO BY BRYAN MCCAY

This brooch is attractive to me because of its **natural structure** that resembles the ovaries of plants or corals. The brooch has **timeless validity** for me. ■ *Pavel Herynek*

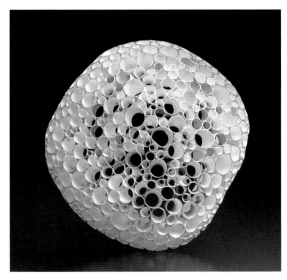

ANYA PINCHUK
Brooch | 2003
7.6 X 7.6 X 2.5 CM
Silver; soldered
PHOTO BY ARTIST

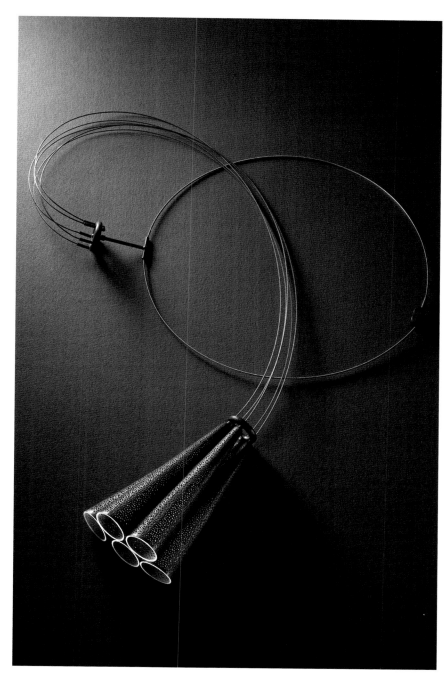

SANDRA ENTERLINE

Five-Cone Drop Pendant | 2008

EACH ELEMENT: 7.6 X 2.2 CM;
NECKLACE: 45 CM LONG

Sterling silver, stainless steel cable; oxidized

PHOTOS BY MARK JOHANN

This necklace makes me think of every piece of ancient gold I have looked at, combined together. It has a very **timeless quality** to it. It looks as if it could have been made in the Middle Ages or today, which I think is very difficult to achieve. I admire the **technical challenges** involved in its creation. I wish I had discovered it buried in the sand on a sunny day in the Mediterranean. That would be finding a real treasure! ■ *Daphne Krinos*

JACQUELINE RYAN
Untitled | 2001

85 CM LONG

18-karat gold, enamel;
hand fabricated

PHOTO BY ARTIST

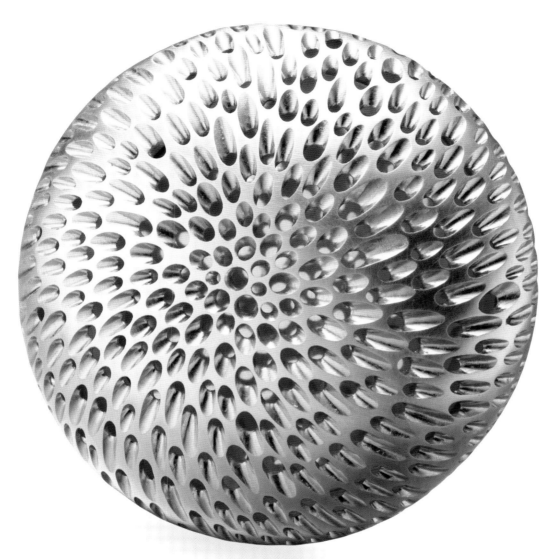

HEATHER BAYLESS
Look and See III | 2008
5 X 5 X 2 CM
Sterling silver, 24-karat gold plating,
mirror; cast, plated, fabricated
PHOTO BY KWANG-CHOON PARK

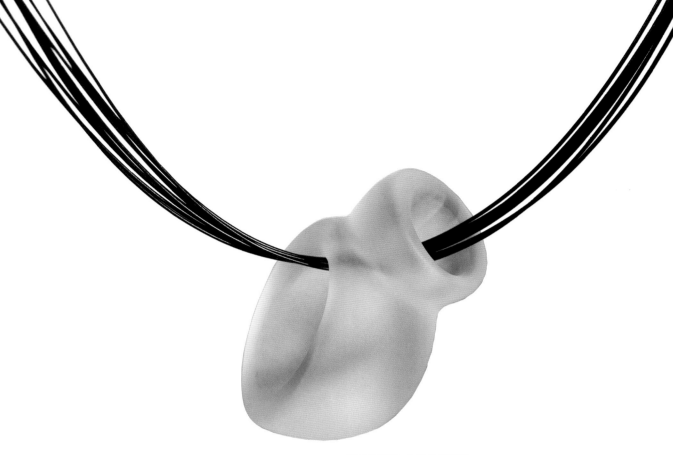

DIETER LORENZ
Carved Citrine Pendant | 2007
1.9 X 3.1 X 1.9 CM
Citrine, elephant hair; carved
PHOTO BY LICHTBLICK PHOTODESIGN

This ring is **perfectly proportioned** both for the eye and for the finger. It has a **sensation and story** on its interior and exterior at the same time. The color of the 22-karat gold carries the form. It must be wonderful to touch and wear! *Castello Hansen*

CHRISTA LÜHTJE
Ring | 2002
2.6 X 1.2 CM
22-karat gold
PHOTO BY EVA JÜNGER

CHRISTA LÜHTJE
Untitled | 2003
6.7 CM IN DIAMETER
22-karat gold, rock crystal
PHOTO BY EVA JÜNGER

To wear this bracelet would **warm the soul** and would be a constant source of **intrigue**. The rich color of the high-karat gold glowing through the rock crystal is lovely. The artist's fine attention to detail, such as the soft rounding of the inner edge for comfort and the hidden clasp, makes this piece **uniquely sophisticated**. *Gina Pankowski*

Refined lines. First realized in two-dimensional sketches that transform and become three-dimensional wearable objects. Funaki's exploration of special relations results in such **pure, beautiful, and timeless** forms. ▪ *Sim Luttin*

This set of three rings is exquisite! I enjoy the way they are folded and formed to create pieces **evocative** of something from nature. The **purity** of the gold is reflected in the **detail** of the inner and outer folded forms. I imagine the feel of the ring on my finger.

▪ *Julie Blyfield*

MARI FUNAKI
Rings | 2000
LARGEST, 2.8 X 2.8 X 1.5 CM
22-karat gold; fabricated
PHOTO BY TERENCE BORGUE

A perfect geometric shape that **emphasizes the form** when it's worn on the finger.
▪ *Sigurd Bronger*

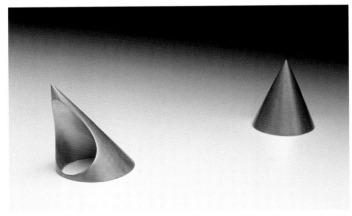

VISINTIN GRAZIANO
Rings | 1981
LEFT, 2.5 X 3 CM; RIGHT, 2.6 X 3 CM
Yellow gold
PHOTO BY LORENZO TRENTO

By my taste, Giovanni Corvaja is the best goldsmith working today, and this bracelet is just one of his many masterpieces. It combines a **structural counterpoint** to the **stunning delicacy** of the fine gold tangles of wire held within it. I'm in awe of Giovanni's skill and sensitivity. ■ *Donald Friedlich*

GIOVANNI CORVAJA
Untitled | 1999

9 X 9 X 4.5 CM

18-karat gold, 22-karat gold, niello; constructed

PHOTO BY ARTIST

DEBORRAH DAHER

Red, White, and Blue Earrings | 2002

EACH, 3.8 X 1.3 X 0.5 CM

22-karat gold, 18-karat gold, lapis lazuli,
garnet, pearl; hand fabricated

PHOTO BY ARTIST

The deepest blue lapis lazuli is the **perfect complement** to artist Mary Lee Hu's exquisite collection of **finely patterned forms**. The design hints at symmetry but on closer inspection you discover each element is a **unique composition** of twined patterns **beautifully crafted** in gold. Wearing this piece could transport you in time to Egypt and a pharaoh's kingdom. ■ *Gina Pankowski*

MARY LEE HU
Choker #82 | 1997
17.5 X 17.5 X 2.5 CM
14-karat gold, 18-karat gold, 22-karat gold,
lapis lazuli; twined, fabricated
PHOTO BY DOUG YAPLE
PRIVATE COLLECTION

CHRIS PLOOF

Meteorite Ring | 2006

2.3 X 2.3 X 0.6 CM

Gibeon meteorite, 18-karat yellow
gold; forged, fabricated, etched

PHOTO BY ROBERT DIAMANTE

Long before meeting Nina, I was attracted to her designs. Her **respect** for the materials she works with always comes across so clearly. Her *Rock Candy Rings* remind me of the cocktail-style rings of years ago but with a **contemporary minimalism** that I relate to distinctly. With this minimalism comes the absolute necessity of **clean workmanship**, and she doesn't disappoint. ▪ *Janis Kerman*

NINA BASHAROVA
Rock Candy Rings | 2006
EACH, 3 X 2.2 X 1.5 CM
18-karat gold, diamonds, tourmaline, peridot
PHOTO BY NAOYA FUJISHIRO

This ring speaks to me because of the material. I love the **juxtaposition** of the cut diamonds with the rough diamond cubes, as well as the large octahedron used as the focal point. It really **celebrates** the material of diamond in all of its wonderful forms. ■ *Geoffrey D. Giles*

TODD REED
Untitled | 2007
1.2 X 1.3 CM
18-karat gold, diamonds;
hand forged, fabricated
PHOTO BY HAP SAKWA

Kent's beautiful **interpretation** and **vision** and his **flawless technique** come together to form a piece that is greater than the sum of its parts.

■ *Michael Good*

KENT RAIBLE
Floating City #6 | 2005
5 X 3.5 X 2.5 CM
18-karat yellow gold, platinum, chalcedony, diamonds, precious stones, semiprecious stones; fabricated, granulation
PHOTO BY HAP SAKWA

The red colors and rough textures make this piece feel like a **molten-hot Aboriginal sun disk**. The rough diamond even looks like it's melting. It needs the blue aqua just to cool off. A very hot piece. ■ *George Sawyer*

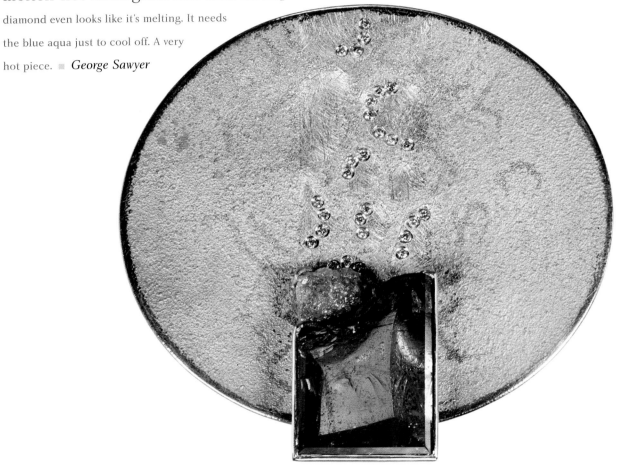

MICHAEL ZOBEL
Brooch/Pendant | 2008
6.5 X 7 X 1.5 CM
18-karat rose gold, platinum, aquamarine, raw diamond; fused
PHOTO BY FRED THOMAS

There is such an **elegant and subtle** beauty in this piece. I respond to the strong curve offset by the delicate granulation. The gold granulation accentuates the curve in an unpredictable manner. The piece feels very **genuine and distinct**.

Sue Amendolara

GIOVANNI CORVAJA

Brooch | 2000

6 X 6 X 1 CM

Platinum, fine gold; granulation

PHOTO BY ARTIST

THE JURORS

Nanz Aalund

Nanz Aalund taught jewelry and metals classes at the University of Washington under Mary Lee Hu and at the Art Institute in Seattle, Washington. She has served as a fine-jewelry designer and consultant for Nordstrom, Rudolf Erdel, Neiman Marcus, and Tiffany & Co., and as the associate editor for *Art Jewelry Magazine*. Some of Aalund's many professional jewelry design awards include a 2009 Jewelry Arts Award, an AGTA Spectrum Award, two Platinum Guild International Awards, and two DeBeers Diamond's Today Awards.

Sue Amendolara

Sue Amendolara received a MFA in jewelry design/metalsmithing from Indiana University, Bloomington, Indiana. She teaches jewelry/metals at Edinboro University of Pennsylvania, Edinboro, Pennsylvania. She is president-elect of the Society of North American Goldsmiths. Her work has been featured in *American Craft*, *Metalsmith*, and *Ornament* magazines, and has been exhibited nationally and internationally. She has received three Individual Artist Fellowships from the Pennsylvania Council on the Arts and a Mid-Atlantic/ NEA Regional Fellowship. Her work is in the permanent collections of the Victoria and Albert Museum, London, England, The Renwick Gallery of the Smithsonian American Art Museum, Washington, D.C., and the White House Collection of American Crafts, Washington, D.C.

Anastasia Azure

Anastasia was first introduced to jewelry fabrication in high school. She continued her training at the Revere Academy of Jewelry Arts, San Francisco, California. While earning her BFA from California College of the Arts, Oakland, California, in 2005, she began practicing jewelry weaving. She completed a three-year residency at the Appalachian Center for Craft, Smithville, Tennessee, that was dedicated to the development of her original dimensional-weave jewelry. Presently, she resides in Providence, Rhode Island, where she is completing her MFA at the Rhode Island School of Design, Providence, Rhode Island. She exhibits nationally as well as internationally.

Talya Baharal

Born in Israel, Talya Baharal made her way to London, England, eventually settling in New York City in the late seventies. Through television commercial production and broadcast journalism at CBS News in both Tel Aviv and New York, her circuitous route to jewelry design was discovered. Smitten by jewelry design via an adult education course taken in New York, she is primarily a self-taught jeweler and sculptor. In collaboration with her husband, Gene Gnida, she formed Baharal-Gnida Designs, a well respected and award-winning collection of studio jewelry represented across the United States and abroad. Talya received a New York Foundation for the Arts Fellowship in 2007 for her *Urban Landscape* and *Residue* series and was awarded grants from the Mid Atlantic Foundation and Women's Studio Workshop in New York for her sculpture. Talya served as juror of the Lark Craft's book *500 Silver Jewelry Designs*, and her work has been published in several contemporary art-jewelry publications. Her work is represented by leading art-jewelry galleries in the United States, where she has had many solo shows.

Ralph Bakker

Born in 1958, Ralph Bakker started out with the thorough training of the Dutch Vocational School for Jewelry in Schoonhoven, Netherlands, followed by education at the Rietveld Academy in Amsterdam, Netherlands, where he graduated in 1994. His jewelry combines a contemporary style with a classic flavor, expressed in sculptural shapes, repetitive elements, and great care for surface and color. Ralph has exhibited at Galerie Louise Smit, Amsterdam, Netherlands; Galerie Slavik, Vienna, Austria; Klimt, Barcelona, Spain; and at Charon Kransen, New York, New York. His work is represented in several private collections and in museums around the world.

Nina Basharova

Art has been Nina Basharova's lifetime passion, and jewelry design has been her occupation for the past 20 years. She received her formal art education in Russia, and completed her studies at WIZO Art Academy in Israel, where she won her first award and a scholarship as a gifted student. She moved to New York, New York in 2002, and started her eponymous collection in 2007, which won more than 16 awards. Having creativity and a sense of humor as guides in her design process, Nina Basharova is on the perpetual quest of perfecting her art.

Harriete Estel Berman

Harriete Estel Berman received her BFA from Syracuse University, Syracuse, New York, and a MFA from Tyler School of Art, Temple University, Philadelphia, Pennsylvania, both with majors in metalsmithing. Since then she has exhibited regularly in the United States and Europe, including seven solo shows. In addition to teaching and giving workshops and lectures, her work is in 13 public collections, including the Museum of Fine Arts, Boston, Massachusetts; Detroit Institute of Arts, Detroit, Michigan; the Renwick Gallery, Smithsonian American Art Museum, Washington, D.C.; and the Jewish Museum, Berlin, Germany. She is featured in more than 31 books, and is the author of *Professional Guidelines* found at www.harriete-estel-berman.info/profguidelines/profguide.html.

Melanie Bilenker

In 2000, Melanie received a BFA in crafts, with a concentration in jewelry and metalsmithing from the University of the Arts in Philadelphia, Pennsylvania, where she resides, creating one-of-a-kind jewelry and works on paper.

Nisa Blackmon

Nisa Blackmon is an artist and biologist hybrid. Her works of art and craft explore and answer questions brought about by science and natural history. She is fascinated by jewelry's cultural history and the seminal role it plays in our lives. She marvels in its connections to identity, power, and the natural world. Nisa encourages her curiosities and interests to work and play together, both in her home studio and at her job in the biology department of Illinois Wesleyan University, Bloomington, Illinois.

Julie Blyfield

Julie runs her own independent studio and is represented by Gallery Funaki in Melbourne, Australia, and Galerie Ra in Amsterdam, Netherlands. Julie exhibits her work internationally with Charon Kransen Arts, New York, New York. Her work is displayed in all of the Australian museum collections, as well as internationally at the Musée des Arts Decoratifs in Paris, France, and the Victoria and Albert Museum in London, England. A survey of her work from 1990–2010 has been presented in an exhibition at FORM Gallery in Perth, Western Australia, and JamFactory Contemporary Craft and Design, Adelaide, South Australia.

Michael Boyd

Michael's work is a compilation of basic metal fabrication and lapidary techniques. His influences are varied and wide. A large part of Michael's work is an exploration of color, using a variety of natural materials consisting mainly of stone. If he had to choose one influence, it would be natural form and pattern in hard-edged, linear structures, of which metal fabrication tends to lean.

Sigurd Bronger

Exhibitions: Lillehammer Art Museum, Lillehammer, Norway, 2011; Nasjonal Museum, Stockholm, Sweden, 2005; Galerie RA, Amsterdam, 1999 and 2006.

Collections: Stedelijk Museum, Amsterdam, Netherlands; Middlesbrough Institute of Modern Art, Middlesbrough, United Kingdom; Design Museum, Helsinki, Finland; National Museum of Art, Architecture, and Design, Oslo, Norway; Victoria and Albert Museum, London, England.

Awards: Norwegian Design Award, 2010; Norwegian Craft Award, 1995; Norwegian Goldsmith Award, 2001

Klaus Burgel

Klaus Burgel received his training at the Akademie der Bildenden Künste in Munich, Germany, and at the Goldschmiedeschule, Pforzheim, Germany. He has had solo exhibitions at Oliver Art Center, California College of Arts and Crafts, Oakland, California; Bernard Toale Gallery, Boston, Massachusetts; Goethe Institut, Boston, Massachusetts; and Jewelerswerk Gallery, Washington D.C. His most recent group shows include *The Fat Booty of Madness*, the International Design Museum, Munich, Germany; *Adornment*, Goucher College, Baltimore, Maryland; *Micromegas*, American Craft Museum, New York, New York; *Historical Connnections*, Mobilia Gallery, Cambridge, Massachusetts; *Art of Gold*, Crocker Art Museum, Sacramento, California; *ICE*, Sienna/Heller Gallery, New York, New York. Prior teaching includes: New York University, New York, New York, the Maine College of Art, Portland, Maine; Rhode Island School of Design, Providence, Rhode Island; UMass Dartmouth, Dartmouth, Massachusetts; California College of Arts, Oakland, California; School of the Museum of Fine Arts, Boston, Massachusetts; and Parsons School of Design, New York, New York. He lives and works in New York, New York.

Jessica Calderwood

Jessica Calderwood is an assistant professor of art at the University of Wisconsin-Oshkosh, Oshkosh, Wisconsin. She received her BFA from the Cleveland Institute of Art, Cleveland, Ohio, and her MFA from Arizona State University, Temple, Arizona, with an emphasis in metalworking. Her work has been displayed in curated and juried exhibitions nationally and internationally. She has participated in artist residencies with the John Michael Kohler Arts Center/Industry Residency Program, Sheboygan, Wisconsin, and the Mesa Arts Center, Mesa, Arizona. Her work has been published in *Metalsmith*, *American Craft*, *NICHE*, and *Ornament* magazines, as well as *The Art of Enameling* (Lark Crafts) and several of the Lark Crafts 500 series books.

Namu Cho

Namu Cho was born in Seoul, Korea, in 1955. Namu earned a BA in 1982 and an MFA in 1984 from Kook-Min University, Seoul, Korea. In 1986, he received his second MFA from Bowling Green State University, Bowling Green, Ohio. He has taught at several universities in Korea, as well as in the United States. Since 1999, Namu Cho has operated Studio Namu, his own limited edition, art-jewelry business in Bethesda, Maryland. He and his wife Jean live with their children Kyle and Jada. He exhibits at crafts shows nationally and has won several awards and prizes for his work. His most distinguished award is the Tiffany Foundation Award, which he received in 1995.

Barbara Cohen

Barbara's formal artistic biography began in 1973 at Sheridan College's School of Design in Oakville, Ontario, where she majored in textiles. For the next 18 years, Barbara created three-dimensional fiber pieces, but later transitioned from sculptural textiles to body ornament, which seemed to be a logical development representing a distillation of artistic focus. She finds inspiration for her creations in the materials that draw her close. Barbara's work consistently uses these found materials out of context to give her pieces an ambiguity that draws the viewer's attention and questions preconceived notions of value to suggest a new meaning.

Cappy Counard

Cappy Counard holds a MFA from Southern Illinois University in Carbondale, Illinois, and a BS in art from the University of Wisconsin-Madison, Madison, Wisconsin. She teaches jewelry and metalsmithing at Edinboro University of Pennsylvania in Edinboro, Pennsylvania. From 2006 to 2009, her work traveled throughout Europe and the United States with the exhibition, *Challenging the Chatelaine*. Cappy's work has also been included in several Lark Crafts publications, including *500 Pendants and Lockets*, *500 Wedding Rings*, *500 Earrings*, and *500 Metal Vessels*. She was the recipient of Pennsylvania Council on the Arts Individual Artist Fellowships in 2003 and 2007.

Lisa and Scott Cylinder

Lisa and Scott Cylinder are a working, collaborative husband and wife team. The Cylinders work with found objects, often disguising and manipulating their original form. They are informed by nature, modernism, and history.

Donna D'Aquino

Donna D'Aquino received her BS in design in 1989 from the State University College of New York at Buffalo, Buffalo, New York. In 2000, she received her MFA in jewelry/metalsmithing from Kent State University, Kent, Ohio. Her work has been exhibited both nationally and internationally.

Deborrah Daher

Deborrah Daher is an internationally published, award-winning artist. Originally a painter and ceramic artist, she fell in love with the art of jewelry making in 1980, bringing her appreciation for color and texture with her.

Charlotte De Syllas

Charlotte was born in 1946 in Barbados, West Indies. She trained under Gerda Flöckinger from 1963 to 1966, and, until five years ago, worked mostly freelance on commission. She now sells her work through Electrum Gallery in London, England and takes commissions. Charlotte works primarily with carved gemstones and metal, and her pieces can be found in several private collections, as well as the permanent collection at the Victoria & Albert Museum in London, England. She has won several awards, including the Jerwood Prize in 1995 and a scholarship from the Queen Elizabeth Scholarship Trust in 1999.

Peter Deckers

Peter Deckers was born in the Netherlands, where he also completed his early jewelry training and art education. He immigrated to New Zealand in 1985 and received an MFA in 2003 from the Elam School of Fine Arts, Auckland University, Auckland, New Zealand. Peter works as a part-time senior art lecturer and coordinator at Whitireia in Porirua, New Zealand, and has curated challenging group exhibitions such as *Jewellery Out of Context* and *HandStand*. He is equal parts contemporary artist and craftsperson. The inspiration for his work comes from the ideas that make distinctive connections with jewelry. His 20-year survey exhibition has highlighted his interest in language through a series of engaging pieces displayed with accompanying sound.

Cindy Edelstein

Cindy Edelstein is the founder and president of the Jeweler's Resource Bureau, a niche consulting company specializing in the designer sector. Cindy is an award-winning writer and entrepreneur, who has helped countless design entrepreneurs grow their businesses. She has worked with artisans, designers, manufacturers, trade associations, publications, trade shows, and government organizations, both in the United States and abroad. Cindy's company connects designers to the industry-at-large online via jewelrydesignerfinder.com and in person at her globalDESIGN show and her work with Couture and the JA NY shows. Her business coaching, seminars, and online social networking help to keep designers learning and progressing with their businesses.

Beate Eismann

From 1990 to 1995, Beate studied jewelry at the Burg Giebichenstein, University of Arts and Design in Halle, Germany, where she also served as an artistic assistant in the Department of Jewellry from 2000 to 2006. After receiving a scholarship from the Carl Duisberg Association, she worked and studied abroad in Mexico City, Mexico from 1995 to 1997. She has freelanced since 1998, as well as lectured at the Staatliche Zeichenakademie in Hanau, Germany. Beate is a scholarship holder of the Art Foundation of the Federal State of Saxony-Anhalt, Germany.

Suzanne Esser

Born in 1946 to a sculptor mother, Suzanne's love for sculptural shapes came naturally. Her work of forms and shapes has been inspired by travels to Mexico and India. She lives and works in Amsterdam, Netherlands, where she also regularly exhibits her work in addition to exhibitions abroad.

Arline M. Fisch

Arline M. Fisch, San Diego State University Professor of Art Emerita, San Diego, California, is an artist and jeweler working primarily in precious metals, exhibiting work nationally and internationally. She is the author of the book *Textile Techniques in Metal* (Lark Crafts), and she frequently conducts intensive, short-term workshops in the United States and abroad. She has lectured and exhibited widely in North America, Europe, and the Far East, and her work is represented in numerous museums and private collections.

Donald Friedlich

Donald Friedlich received his BFA from Rhode Island School of Design, Providence, Rhode Island, in 1982. He served as president of the Society of North American Goldsmiths and also chair of the *Metalsmith* magazine editorial committee. His jewelry is in the permanent collections of the Victoria and Albert Museum, London, England; the Smithsonian American Art Museum, Washington D.C.; the Museum of Fine Arts, Boston, Massachusetts; the Schmuckmuseum, Pforzheim, Germany; the Corning Museum of Glass, Corning, New York; the Museum of Fine Arts, Houston, Texas; and others. He has been an artist-in-residence at The Studio of the Corning Museum of Glass, Corning, New York, Australian National University, Canberra, Australia; and Tainan National School of Art, Tainan, Taiwan.

Geoffrey D. Giles

Working primarily in 18-karat gold, Geoffrey Giles creates one-of-a-kind, limited edition jewelry. Geoffrey's work has been exhibited both nationally and internationally, and has been featured in numerous publications. Throughout his career, Geoffrey has received a range of honors within his field, and is a member of the American Jewelry Design Council, whose mission is to promote the appreciation of original jewelry design as art.

Joanna Gollberg

Joanna Gollberg is a studio jeweler in Asheville, North Carolina. In addition to making jewelry, she is the author of four Lark Crafts books: *Making Metal Jewelry*;

Creative Metal Crafts; The Art and Craft of Making Jewelry; and *The Ultimate Jeweler's Guide.* Joanna teaches jewelry making for metalsmithing groups across the country, as well as craft schools such as Penland School of Crafts. She exhibits her work at fine craft shows and galleries nationally.

Michael Good

Born in Pittsburgh, Pennsylvania, of Belgian parents, Michael Good is primarily a self-taught jeweler and sculptor. He is known around the world as "the Father of Anticlastic Raising." He has been a goldsmith and teacher since 1969, and has taught workshops for professional organizations, schools, and universities in North America and Europe. His work is represented in stores, galleries, and private collections around the globe. His studio is located in a converted, 100-year-old barn in Rockport, Maine, a traditional New England seacoast community.

Caroline Gore

Overall, Caroline Gore's work is a simple reflection of the everyday. She turns contemplative moments into tangible forms that take on a part of her experience and life process. While maintaining an active studio practice, she is an associate professor of art and area coordinator for the metals/jewelry program at Western Michigan University in Kalamazoo, Michigan. Her work is currently represented by Ornamentum Gallery in Hudson, New York.

Rebecca Hannon

Rebecca completed her undergraduate degree at Rhode Island School of Design, Providence, Rhode Island, in 1995, and went on to work as a professional goldsmith in New York, New York. After a thorough professional education, she decided it was time to focus solely on her practice, and applied to study under Otto Künzli at the Akademie der Bildenden Künste in Munich, Germany. She studied, taught, and eventually became a member of a professional jewelry collective in Germany from 2000 to 2005 with support from a Fulbright grant. She now maintains her own workshop, participates in international exhibitions, and teaches full-time at the Nova Scotia College of Art and Design University in Halifax, Novia Scotia.

Hanna Hedman

Hanna was born in 1980 in Stockholm, Sweden. She has studied in Sweden, the United States, and New Zealand, and graduated with a master's degree in 2008 from Konstfack in Stockholm, Sweden, studying under professors Ruudt Peters and Karen Pontoppidan. She had her first solo exhibition in 2009. Her work is on display at museums and in private collections in Europe and the United States. In her work, she includes fantasy, reality, art, and function, derived from inspiration found in human weakness, darkness, nature, and storytelling. She draws interest in the contrasts between beauty and the unpleasant.

Castello Hansen

Goldsmith

MA, Royal College of Art, London, England

Professor, HDK, University of Gothenburg, Gothenburg, Sweden, 2004 to 2007

Thomas Herman

Classically trained at the Van Creaynest factory in San Francisco, California, Tom Herman has been making and designing jewelry for more than 30 years. His love of nature is seen in every piece he makes, from the stone cutting to the carving of the gold. He sells his work through museum and craft shows and by appointment.

Pavel Herynek

Pavel lives in Olomouc, Czech Republic. His focus is on drawing, jewelry, and object making. He studied at the School of Applied Arts in Brno, Czech Republic, and at Palack University in Olomouc, Czech Republic, where he also taught 3-D art courses from 1990 to 2003. In 1994, he founded and became head of the Metal and Jewelry Studio. His works are represented in collections in the Czech Republic, as well as abroad.

Thomas Hill

Thomas Hill trained as a jeweler at Middlesex University in London, England. In 1994, he set up a studio, and has since worked as a full-time studio artist. He is best known for his steel wire sculptures of birds and animals, but he also draws and makes jewelry. Exhibits include the Collect Art Fair at the Saatchi Gallery in London, England; the British Crafts Council at the Victoria and Albert Museum, London, England; and solo shows at Velvet da Vinci, San Francisco, California; and the Fuller Craft Museum, Brockton, Massachusetts. He has undertaken a number of public commissions, including the BBC Symphony Orchestra, the Hyatt Hotel Group, and the John Lewis Partnership.

Leonor Hipólito

Leonor graduated from the Gerrit Rietveld Academy in Amsterdam, Netherlands, in 1999. In 1998, he attended the Parson's School of Design in New York, New York, as an exchange student. He was an Artist in Residence at the University of Applied Sciences-Trier, in Idar-Oberstein, Germany, 2008. Since 1999, Leonor has lived and worked as an independent artist and teacher in Lisbon, Portugal, and, since 1998, has been exhibiting work in individual and group shows in Portugal and abroad.

Mike Holmes

Mike's training is in jewelry and metalwork, and since 1991, he has been the co-owner of Velvet da Vinci, San Francisco, California, a gallery specializing in contemporary jewelry. Mike is also on the board of directors of the Art Jewelry Forum.

Mary Lee Hu

Mary Lee Hu studied metalsmithing and jewelry at Rochester Institute of Technology in Rochester, New York, with Hans Christensen. She received a BFA from the Cranbrook Academy of Art, Bloomfield Hills, Michigan, with Richard Thomas in 1965, and a MFA from Southern Illinois University-Carbondale, Carbondale, Illinois, with Brent Kington in 1967. She taught at Michigan State University, East Lansing, Michigan, from 1977 to 1980, and at the University of Washington-Seattle, Seattle, Washington, from 1980 until her retirement in 2006. She served as president of the Society of North American Goldsmiths from 1977 to 1980. Her jewelry, primarily made with twined wires, has been exhibited internationally, and is in many major museum collections. She has had a long-standing interest in traditional body adornment, particularly that of Asian cultures.

Chris Irick

Chris Irick is a professor of metal arts at Pratt MWP in Utica, New York. Her work has been featured in numerous Lark Crafts publications including *500 Pendants & Lockets*; *500 Brooches*; *500 Bracelets*; *The Art and Craft of Making Jewelry*; and *The Penland Book of Jewelry*, as well as *Metalsmith* and *American Craft* magazines, and the book *The Metalsmith's Book of Boxes and Lockets*. Her work has been exhibited nationally, and is included in the permanent collection of the Smithsonian American Art Museum, Washington D.C.

Nicole Jacquard

Nicole received a BA from Indiana University, Bloomington, Indiana in 1991 and her first MFA from the University of Michigan. She received her second MFA while on a Fulbright Scholarship to Australia, and in 2004, Nicole completed her Ph.D. in Fine Arts at RMIT University in Melbourne, Australia. Since 2005, Nicole has been an assistant professor at Indiana University in Bloomington, Indiana. She has had five solo exhibitions and participated in more than 70 invitational/juried exhibitions. She has presented more than 20 lectures on her work, and her work is published in more than 30 books, catalogues, and websites. Her two solo catalogues are both available through Charon Kransen Arts, New York, New York.

Janis Kerman

Janis Kerman's studio is a renovated coach house a short distance from her home. Her desk is alive with a laptop, a pair of burgundy-framed glasses, colored pencils, clients' notes, and logistics paperwork. Sketches are meticulously ordered and accompanied by the appropriate stones. Clients visiting the studio for commissions participate in the design process, from inception to finished wearable jewelry.

Charon Kransen

Charon Kransen was born in the Netherlands and trained in Germany, Israel, and Norway. He has worked in the field of contemporary jewelry since 1969 as a jeweler, professor, lecturer, curator, art dealer, and agent for nearly 150 international contemporary jewelers at art fairs such as SOFA Chicago, Chicago, Illinois, SOFA New York, New York, and the Miami International Art Fair, Miami, Florida. He has lectured on contemporary jewelry and has given master classes to students and professionals worldwide.

Daphne Krinos

Born in Athens, Greece, Daphne studied at Middlesex University in London, England. She set up her own studio in 1982, and has shown her work in many galleries in the United Kingdom and abroad. Daphne's work belongs to several public and private collections, and is featured in many books published in the United Kingdom and the United States.

Birgit Laken

Birgit Laken lives and works in Haarlem, Netherlands. She studied at the Royal Academy of Art in The Hague, and Gerrit Rietveld Academy, Amsterdam, Netherlands. Her work is characterized by pure, strong lines, and she often develops her work through a themed project, which can evolve and grow over a period of time; this takes her to a deeper understanding of the source that inspired her. By way of several grants, she learned the mokume gane technique and developed her Heartwear and Heartwork projects, including her most recent, *Summerland*.

Deborah Lozier

Deborah Lozier is an internationally known metalsmith, jeweler, enamellist, and instructor. Her studio practice involves an organic and open approach to vitreous enamel on fabricated copper and steel. Students taking her courses learn from her process-driven philosophy of working in the moment. Along with studio jewelry and sculpture, Deborah also creates architectural public and community art pieces. She teaches Color on Metal at California College of the Arts in Oakland, California, and at art institutions throughout the United States and England.

Ann L. Lumsden

Ann L. Lumsden has more than 20 years experience working as a goldsmith and designer. Her work appears in the book *Art Jewelry Today 2*, as well as numerous Lark Crafts publications, including several books in the 500 series and the 30-Minute series. She is a member of the Metal Arts Guild of Canada, where her pieces have twice been named best in show in their annual juried exhibitions. She lives and works in Ottawa, Ontario, Canada.

Sim Luttin

In 2003, Sim Luttin received a BFA in gold and silversmithing from RMIT University, Melbourne, Australia, and in 2008, received her masters in metalsmithing and jewelry design from Indiana University, Bloomington, Indiana. Significant exhibitions include *By Example*, *Australian Contemporary Jewellery* the Museum of Arts and Crafts, Itami, Japan, 2010; *Hint of a Memory*, Metalab, Sydney, Australia, 2009; and *The Temporary Nature of Things*, Pieces of Eight Gallery, Melbourne, Australia, 2008. Sim was the recipient of the Alma Eikerman Award for Metalsmithing, 2008. She is included in collections at Galerie Marzee, Nijmegen, The Netherlands, and the Art Gallery of South Australia, Adelaide, Australia.

Linda MacNeil

Inspired by ancient and modern history, Linda MacNeil challenges accepted wisdom among connoisseurs of fine jewelry with compositions in glass and metal. MacNeil's jewelry and sculpture can be found worldwide in galleries, private collections, and prestigious museums, most notably the Metropolitan Museum of Art, New York, New York, the Victoria and Albert Museum, London, England, and the Museum of Fine Art, Boston, Massachusetts.

Mia Maljojoki

Mia was born and raised in Joensuu, Finland. In 2001, she received a BFA in small metals from the Massachusetts College of Art and Design, Boston, Massachusetts. In 2004, she worked as project manager for the Contact jewelry symposium, workshop, and exhibition, bringing artists from six different countries. In 2004, she continued her studies at the Academy of Fine Arts in Munich, Germany, under Professor Otto Künzli. Since 2006, she has worked with the Finnish Embassy in Berlin to bring Finnish jewelry artists to Munich, Germany, to exhibit during Internationale Handwerk Messe and Schmuck. In 2010, Mia received the Herbert Hofmann Award at Schmuck, as well as her diploma degree as a meisterschulerin. Her work is currently displayed at Gallery Spektrum, Munich, Germany; Gallery Rob Goudijs, Amsterdam, The Netherlands; and Gallery Noel Guyomarc'h, Montreal, Canada. Mia lives and works in Munich, Germany, with her husband and two children.

Stefano Marchetti

1984–1989 Istituto Statale d'Arte "Pietro Selvatico," Padova, Italy

1990–1994, Academy of Fine Arts in Venice, Italy

1994–1996; 2007–2010, teacher at Istituto Statale d'Arte "Pietro Selvatico," Padova, Italy

Prizes: 1994 Bayerischer Staatpreis, München, Talentepreis, München; 2001 Premio di incentivazione Internova 2001, Bolzano; 2009 Italian Jewellery Awards, Napoli

Public Collections: Musée des Arts Décoratifs, Paris, France; Museum voor Moderne Kunst, Arnhem, Netherlands; Landesmuseum Joanneum, Graz, Austria; Fonds National d'Art Contemporain, Paris, France; National Museum of Scotland, Edinburgh, Scotland; Museum für Kunst und Gewerbe, Hamburg, Germany; Museum of Arts and Design, New York, New York; Marzee Collection, Nijmegen, Netherlands; Schmuckmuseum Pforzheim, Pforzheim, Germany; the Alice and Louis Koch Collection, Basel, Switzerland; Museo degli Argenti, Palazzo Pitti, Florence, Italy.

Wendy McAllister

Wendy McAllister is an independent studio jeweler who made sculptural ceramic objects before graduating with a major in jewelry design from the Maryland Institute College of Art in Baltimore, Maryland. Her one-of-a-kind enameled brooches reference the natural world and its underlying, elegant geometry and quirky technicolor surfaces. Her work is exhibited with Charon Kransen Arts at the SOFA exhibitions in New York, Chicago, Illinois, and Santa Fe, New Mexico.

Tom Muir

Tom Muir is Distinguished Research Professor at Bowling Green State University, Bowling Green, Ohio, where he is the head of jewelry and metalsmithing

in the School of Art. His award-winning work has been published and exhibited extensively in art, craft, and design exhibitions, in which he has received 10 best-of-show or first-place awards. His work is represented in numerous public collections and, in 2009, Tom received the Outstanding Achievement Award from the Ohio Designer Craftsmen for having made a major contribution to craft in Ohio.

Tom Munsteiner

Born in Bernkastel-Kues, Germany, in 1969, Tom was educated as a lapidary stone-cutter from 1985 to 1989 by Bernd Munsteiner. In 1991, he received his education as a gemologist, and from 1993 to 1995 he studied gemstone and jewelry design in Idar-Oberstein, Germany. Tom became a master of gemstone cutting in 1995, and since 1997, has been with an atelier in Stipshausen, Germany.

Gurhan Orhan

Gurhan is a renowned international jewelry designer, known for pioneering the revival of pure 24-karat gold jewelry. Gurhan showcases his passion for unusual metals, not only with pure 24-karat gold, but with pure platinum, silver, bronze, and, most recently, his revolutionary new 4/24 gold. Gurhan's signature technique, inspired by the art of ancient goldsmiths, offers extraordinary craftsmanship in every piece. His combination of exceptional design and remarkable workmanship attracts leading international retailers, as well as royalty and celebrities, such as Angelina Jolie, Queen Rania of Jordan, and Sandra Bullock.

emiko oye

emiko oye is a San Francisco artist who works in recycled and repurposed materials such as LEGO®, circuit boards, and industrial plastics and scraps. Inspired by hardware, haute couture, and salvaged materials, emiko creates one-of-a-kind urban jewelry and conceptual sculptures. She strives to subtly transform the identity of everyday mundane objects to create new dialogues about our relationships with the environment and our culture. Active in the Bay Area art community, emiko is on the board of directors for the Metal Arts Guild. She facilitates community recycled jewelry projects through her Accessorize with Toys workshops, and frequently gives lectures on how to survive as an artist. Her work is shown in museums and galleries across the United States and Europe, and is featured at the Museum of Contemporary Craft, Portland, Oregon.

Barbara Paganin

Born in 1961, Paganin studied goldsmithing at the Istituto Statale d'Arte in Venice, Italy, where she now teaches design. In 1980, she earned a degree in sculpture at the Accademia di Belle Arti in Venice, Italy. Working primarily with gold, silver, glass, and diamonds, Barbara creates jewelry that openly references nature, particularly the plant kingdom. She has taken part in several national and international exhibitions, and, in 2002, she lectured at the Royal College of Art in London, England. Her work is on display in leading museums around the world, including the Metropolitan Museum of Art, New York, New York.

Gina Pankowski

As an artist, Gina has an eye for pattern and a deep love of nature and technology. Born in the northwest, United States, she has degrees in metal design, sculpture, and art history from the University of Washington, Seattle, Washington. Gina's work has been exhibited and published internationally, and is featured in several public collections, including the Renwick Gallery at the Smithsonian American Art Museum, Washington, D.C. She loves traveling, gardening, and spending time with her children.

Seth Papac

Seth Papac graduated with his BFA in 2004 from the University of Washington, Seattle, Washington, and received his MFA in 2009 from the Cranbrook Academy of Art, Bloomfield Hills, Michigan. His work is seen internationally in galleries and exhibitions, and can be found in the permanent collections of the Museum of Contemporary Craft, Portland, Oregon; the Cranbrook Art Museum, Bloomfield Hills, Michigan; the Tacoma Art Museum, Tacoma, Washington; and the Rotasa Foundation, Mill Valley, California.

Mary Hallam Pearse

Mary Hallam Pearse received her MFA in metal from SUNY New Paltz, New Paltz, New York, and her BFA in metals/jewelry from Kent State University, Kent, Ohio. Recent exhibitions of her work include *Materials: Hard & Soft*; *Charmed*; *Paper or Plastic?*; and *CraftForms*. Her work is featured in several Lark Crafts publications, including *500 Gemstone Jewels*; *500*

Pendants & Lockets; and *The Art of Jewelry: Plastic & Resin*. She is represented by J. Cotter Gallery in Vail, Colorado, Heidi Lowe Gallery in Rehoboth Beach, Delaware, and Julie: Artisans' Gallery in New York, New York. Currently she is the assistant professor in metals/jewelry at The University of Georgia, Athens, Georgia.

Ruudt Peters

Ruudt Peters is a pioneering Dutch conceptual jewelry artist that began challenging traditional definitions of adornment in the 1970s by pushing the boundaries of context, wearability, materials, and presentation. A leader in art jewelry in the Netherlands, Peters exemplifies a mode of expression that is unmistakably Dutch. He has had a strong influence on the development of contemporary jewelry as an artist and as a professor at two of the most prestigious universities in Europe: the Gerrit Rietveld Academy in Amsterdam, Netherlands, and Konstfack University of Arts and Crafts in Stockholm, Sweden. Peters is currently a professor at the contemporary jewelry and design school, Alchimia in Florence, Italy.

Natalya Pinchik

In 2001, Natalya received her BFA from Indiana University, Bloomington, Indiana, and her MFA from University of Illinois at Urbana-Champaign, Champaign, Illinois, in 2005. Her jewelry is shown by Charon Kransen Arts at SOFA Chicago, Chicago, Illinois; and SOFA NY, New York, New York; Galerie Rob Koudijs, Amsterdam, Netherlands; and Jewelerswerk Galerie, Washington, D.C. Natalya's jewelry is

in the collections of the Mint Museum of Craft + Design, Charlotte, North Carolina, and Stedelijk Museum, 's-Hertogenbosch, Netherlands.

Beverley Price

Beverly is a sculptor and jewelry artist. Her South African surroundings inspire her pre- and post-colonial apartheid adornment practices, with a South African post-modern hybrid aesthetic. She draws from the semiotics and kinetic wearability of jewelry. Beverley has exhibited nationally and internationally, and her work has been collected and worn throughout the world.

Katja Prins

Katja graduated from the Gerrit Rietveld Academy, Amsterdam, Netherlands, in 1997, and has been working as an independent jewelry designer ever since. She has had solo and group exhibitions all over Europe, the United States, Asia, and Russia. Her work can be found in public collections at Stedelijk Museum, 's-Hertogenbosch, Netherlands; Mint Museum of Craft + Design, Charlotte, North Carolina; and the Schmuckmuseum, Pforzheim, Germany. In 2009, she published her monograph *The Uncanny Valley*, which gives an overview of all her work. She has been a Rotterdam Design Prize nominee, and in 2009, she won the Darling Publications' Jeweler of the Year award.

Todd Reed

Todd Reed is a self-taught goldsmith and jeweler. His affinity for jewelry making started around the age of 10 while on a family vacation in Bisbee, Arizona. After designing furniture and clothes, sculpting, painting, and graduating with honors from culinary school, Todd officially launched a jewelry collection under his own name in 1992 and set out to change jewelry's future by creating solely with raw and uncut diamonds. His work has been featured in many of the finest books on goldsmithing and art jewelry. He has received multiple awards, such as the Town & Country Couture Award in 2008, and has been honored by the American Craft Council and the Society of North American Goldsmiths. For the past two years, Todd has served as president of the board of The American Jewelry Design Council.

George Sawyer

George Sawyer is an American jewelry designer with a particular (or peculiar) interest in creating unique jewelry with multicolored, painterly surfaces. He is the originator of gold mokume and related multicolored, metalworking techniques. His studio workshop is in Minneapolis, Minnesota.

Marjorie K. Schick

Marjorie Schick is a university professor of art at Pittsburg State University in Pittsburg, Kansas, and is recognized for her large-scale jewelry of non-traditional materials. In 2000, she was named a fellow of the American Craft Council, and in 2004, she interviewed for the National Archives of American Art Oral History Program for the Smithsonian Institution, Washington, D.C. Marjorie's work can be seen in museums, including the Victoria & Albert Museum, London, England, and

the Museum of Arts and Design, New York, New York. In 2007, Arnoldsche Art Publishers, Stuttgart, Germany, published the book *Sculpture to Wear: The Jewelry of Marjorie Schick* by Tacey Rosolowski.

Claude Schmitz

Claude completed studies at the Royal Academy of Fine Arts in Antwerp, Belgium, and the Royal College of Art in London, England, and has been working as an independent artist and designer in Luxembourg since 2001. He designs and manufactures jewelry and objects, lectures in Europe and Asia, and has work featured in public and private collections throughout Europe, Asia, and the United States.

Karin Seufert

Education: Gerrit Rietveld Academy, Amsterdam, Netherlands, 1995

Exhibitions: *Jewelry Quake*, Tokyo, Japan, Munich, Germany, Amsterdam, Netherlands, 1993; *Schmuck*, Munich, Germany, 1997; *Micromegas*, Munich, Germany, New York, New York, Tokyo, Japan, 2001; solo exhibition, Gallery Marzee, Nijmegen, Netherlands, 2002 and 2009; *Gold*, Gallery Oona, Berlin, Germany, 2004; *First We Quake Now We Shake*, Amsterdam, Netherlands, Tokyo, Japan, Munich, Germany, Bern, Switzerland, Stockholm, Sweden, Mexico City, Mexico, 2005; solo exhibition, Museum of Applied Arts, Frankfurt, Germany, 2007; solo exhibition, Gallery Hnoss, Gothenburg, Sweden, 2008; Koru 3, Imatra Art Museum, Imatra, Finland, 2009; *Walking the Gray Area*, Mexico City, Mexico, 2010; *Porcelain*, Gallery Hélène Porée, Paris, France, 2010

Susan Kasson Sloan

Susan is a studio jeweler and instructor, and is on the faculty of the 92nd Street Y in New York, New York, and the Art School at the Old Church in Demarest, New Jersey, and teaches workshops nationally. She is the recipient of three New Jersey State Council on the Arts Fellowship grants. Her work is included in the collections of the Victoria & Albert Museum, London, England; the Racine Art Museum, Racine, Wisconsin; the Renwick Gallery Smithsonian American Art Museum, Washington, D.C.; and the Cooper-Hewitt National Design Museum, New York, New York, amongst others.

Fabrizio Tridenti

Graduated: Istituto Statale d'Arte, Penne, Italy

Public Collections: Museo degli Argenti, Palazzo Pitti, Firenze, Italy; Museum of Contemporary Craft, Portland, Oregon, USA; Museum of the Arts, Nocciano Castle, Pescara, Italy; Museo delle Arti e del Multimediale, Micro Art Collection, Petrabbondante, Isernia, Italy.

Selected Solo Exhibitions: *Fabrizio Tridenti, Samples*, Popoli, Italy; *Abruzzo terra di personaggi illustri sculpture*, Pescara, Italy; *Timeless Shape*, Venezia, Italy.

Recent Juried Exhibitions: *II International Meeting of Creative Jewellery With Glass*, Madrid, Spain; *Intimacy*, New Traditional Jewellery Award, Amsterdam, The Netherlands; *New Play in Art*, Gardone Riviera, Italy; *Papierschmuck*, Steyrermuhl, Austria; *Exclusive*, International Silverart Competition, Poland; *Amberif Design Award Elektronos 2008*, Gdansk, Poland; *Touching Warms the Art!*, Portland, Oregon; *Gioiello*

Italiano Contemporaneo, Palazzo Valmarana (Vicenza), Castello Sforzesco (Milan), Museum of Decorative Arts (Torino), Italy, Museum of Applied Arts, Berlin, Germany.

Felieke van der Leest

Felieke van der Leest graduated in 1996 from the jewelry department at the Gerrit Rietveld Academy in Amsterdam, Netherlands, and is a trained metalsmith. She has worked as an artist and designer ever since, making colorful and humorous jewelry and small objects. Her work has been highly regarded in the international jewelry scene for many years, and is featured in museum and private collections around the world. Since 2008, she has lived and worked in the Hardanger, Norway.

Ingeborg Vandamme

Ingeborg studied jewelry design at the Gerrit Rietveld Academy in Amsterdam, Netherlands. Over the years, she has taught jewelry design in workshops and art schools, and her work has been exhibited in galleries in the Netherlands and abroad. A recurring theme in her work is nurtured memories, and she draws inspiration from natural processes, with an attention to imperfection and impermanence through combinations of diverse materials, such as metal, paper, textile, and objects from nature. Her jewelry is featured in numerous publications, including several Lark Crafts books. Ingeborg works and lives in Amsterdam, Netherlands.

Miriam Verbeek

In 1993, Miriam graduated from the jewelry department of the Gerrit Rietveld Academy in Amsterdam, Netherlands, with a collection of mourning jewelry, made with different materials and techniques. Today, her work mainly consists of textiles and natural materials such wool, silk, and that of vegetable origin, which lend themselves to vast opportunities. Inspiration for her work generally comes from nature, Dutch folklore, and her own memories. These days, Miriam does not limit her creativity to jewelry alone. She has started to make objects and wall coverings from handmade felt.

Andrea Wagner

Andrea was born in Germany and grew up in Canada. She studied jewelry at the Gerrit Rietveld Academy, Amsterdam, Netherlands and graduated in 1997. Since 1994, Andrea has owned and operated her own studio in Amsterdam, Netherlands. She served as curator and organizer of the touring exhibition, *Golden Clogs, Dutch Mountains* to seven venues in the United States and Canada from 2007 to 2008. She was the co-curator of the exhibition, *Walking the Gray Area* in Mexico City, Mexico, in 2010. Her work is featured in public and private collections and exhibitions, nationally and internationally. Andrea has been the recipient of several artist stipends and financed projects through organizations such as the Netherlands Foundation for Visual Arts, Design and, Architecture, and the Mondriaan Foundation.

Kathryn Wardill

Kathryn Wardill received her master's from RMIT University, Melbourne, Australia, in 1998. As a jeweler and glass artist, she has actively participated in solo and group exhibitions internationally for the past 15 years. Wardill's research in metal and glass jewelry objects has resulted in a solo exhibition in the United States in 2010, and new work presented at Studio Ingot, Fitzroy, Australia, in August of 2010.

Francis Willemstijn

Francis Willemstijn lives and works in Amsterdam, Netherlands. In 2004, she graduated from the Gerrit Rietveld Academy in Amsterdam, Netherlands. She's had solo and group exhibitions in the Netherlands, Germany, Belgium, United States, Finland, Estonia, England, Portugal, France, Switzerland, and Canada. The inspiration for her jewelry is derived from historical images, which she interprets to form her own contemporary context. As a reaction to our consumer-driven society, dominated by industrial products, she tries to charge her work with a great deal of energy and time, and she wishes to represent the past in her work.

Susan and Jeff Wise

Susan and Jeff Wise have more than 60 years experience as metalsmiths between them, and have exhibited and taught throughout the United States. Their work is in the permanent collection of the Smithsonian Institute, Washington, D.C.; the Museum of Fine Art, Boston, Massachusetts; and the Museum of Art and Design, New York, New York. They live in Durango, Colorado, in a modernist home they built themselves. In addition to metalsmithing, Susan is also a painter and Jeff, a sculptor.

ACKNOWLEDGMENTS

To Robert Ebendorf, who helped inaugurate the 500 series by introducing Lark to jewelers from around the world, I extend my sincere appreciation. A special thanks goes to the jurors whose discernment and expertise have shaped each volume in the series: Talya Baharal, Cindy Edelstein, Mike Holmes, Charon Kransen, Alan Revere, Marjorie Schick, Elizabeth Shypertt, Marjorie Simon, and Susan Kasson Sloan.

This book wouldn't have been possible without the 85 wonderful jewelers who chose the work and contributed comments. I appreciate the thoughtfulness and care they invested in the selection process. The insightful introductions written by Jo Bloxham, Giovanni Corvaja, Ron Porter, Marjorie Schick, Katie Scott, and Mari Shaw provide a wonderful context for the jewelry. I am grateful for the unique perspectives they bring to this volume.

At Lark, I'm indebted to Dawn Dillingham, Abby Haffelt, and Julie Hale for their first-class editorial assistance, and to Kathy Holmes, Shannon Yokeley, and Jessica Yee for their art production expertise. Art director Carol Barnao did a beautiful job of laying out the book. Todd Kaderabek and Lance Wille offered their usual outstanding production support. My thanks to all.

— MARTHE LE VAN

CONTRIBUTING ARTISTS

A

Aalund, Nanz Bellingham, Washington 282

Abrasha San Francisco, California 197

Adam, Jane London, United Kingdom 39

addam Perth, Australia 384

Agor, Vicente San Francisco, California 133

Allison, Fran Grey Lynn
Auckland, New Zealand 303

Amano, Shihoko Rye, New York 98

Amendolara, Suzanne Edinboro,
Pennsylvania 342

Amtsberg, Sabine Isernhagen, Germany 75

Anderson, Marianne Glasgow, Scotland 154

Ataumbi, Keri Santa Fe, New Mexico 166

Auman, Megan Kent, Ohio 125

Ayres, Robin Dallas, Texas 100

Azure, Anastasia Providence,
Rhode Island 117

B

Babetto, Giampaolo Arqua'Petrarca,
Italy 284

Baharal, Talya Rifton, New York 369

Bakker, Ralph Rotterdam, Netherlands 156

Bally, Boris Providence, Rhode Island 269

Barello, Julia M. Las Cruces, New Mexico 61

Barer, Belle Brooke Los Angeles,
California 222

Basharova, Nina New York,
New York 388, 399

Bauer, Ela Amsterdam, Netherlands 28, 200

Bayless, Heather Manhattan,
Kansas 60, 391

Beaver, Jeanne Dexter, Kentucky 383

Bennett, Jamie Lenox, Massachusetts 131

Berman, Harriete Estel San Mateo,
California 268

Betz, Doris Munich, Germany 240

Bielander, David Munich, Germany 256, 327

Bilenker, Melanie Philadelphia,
Pennsylvania 94, 207, 379

Binnion, James E. Bellingham, Washington 148

Björkman, Sofia Enskede, Sweden 63

Blackmon, Nisa Bloomington, Illinois 245

Bloomard, Adrean Rome, Italy 276

Blyfield, Julie Adelaide, Australia 190

Bodemer, Iris Pforzheim, Germany 361

Bolhuis, Kristine Ferndale, Michigan 89

Bone, Allyson New Paltz, New York 335

Bone, Elizabeth London, United Kingdom 182

Bontridder, Thierry
Rhode Saint Genese, Belgium 162

Book, Flora Seattle, Washington 110

Boyd, Michael Pueblo, Colorado 79

Brill, Reina Mia New York, New York 170, 257

Britton, Helen Munich, Germany 294

Bronger, Sigurd Oslo, Norway 261

Brooks, Lola New York, New York 291

Brugger, Monika Paimpont, France 307

Bürgel, Klaus New York, New York 74, 80

Buszkiewicz, Kathy Cleveland Heights,
Ohio 101

Büyükünal, Burcu Erenkoy, Turkey, 180

C

Calderwood, Jessica Menasha, Wisconsin 208

Carberry, Michael Aylesbury,
United Kingdom 186

Catchpole, Bridget Vancouver, Canada 201

Cavalan, Pierre Sydney, Australia 103

Cepka, Anton Sväty Jur, Slovakia 385

Chan, Kai Toronto, Canada 88

Chang, Peter Glasgow,
Scotland 9, 176, 270, 324

Chang, Yuyen Madison, Wisconsin 186, 236

Chavent, Claude Puéchabon, France 52

Cho, Namu Bethesda, Maryland 205

Cho, Sungho Munich, Germany 167

Choi, Seung Hye Providence, Rhode Island 123

Clark, William Berkeley, California 289

Cohen, Barbara Vancouver, Canada 213

Cokus, Patty L. Tukwila, Washington 38

Cooperman, Andy Seattle, Washington 207

Corvaja, Giovanni Todi, Italy 7, 157, 234,
345, 395, 403

Cotter, Jim Vail, Colorado 357

Counard, Cappy Edinboro, Pennsylvania 231

Crespo, Paula Lisboa, Portugal 34

Cuyás, Ramon Puig Vilanova i la Geltru, Spain
179, 306

Cylinder, Lisa Oley, Pennsylvania 250

Cylinder, Scott Oley, Pennsylvania 250

D

D'Aquino, Donna Wallkill, New York 206

Daher, Deborrah St. Louis, Missouri 396

Dahm, Johanna Züerich, Switzerland 192

Davies, Jennaca Leigh North Kingstown,
Rhode Island 30, 142

de Decker, Hilde Merchtem, Belgium 299

de Jong, Rian Amsterdam, Netherlands 128

De Syllas, Charlotte Norwich,
United Kingdom 195

Dean, Tami Portland, Oregon 352

Deckers, Peter Wellington, New Zealand 203

Desjardins, Josée North Hatley, Canada 106

Dilaver, Emre Istanbul, Turkey 152

Dittlmann, Bettina Egglham, Germany 29

Dodd, Jane Opoho, New Zealand 6, 255

Domitrovich, Chuck Seattle, Washington 97

Dudek, Diana Munich, Germany 286

Dunmire, Coco Florence, Italy 180

E

Ebendorf, Robert Greenville,
North Carolina 251

Eberhardt, Angela Cleveland, Ohio 121

Eichenberg, Iris Amsterdam, Netherlands 116

Eid, Cynthia Lexington, Massachusetts 288

Eismann, Beate Halle (Saale), Germany 194

Eitzenhöfer, Ute Karlsruhe, Germany 72

Engelkes, Cathelijne Amsterdam, Netherlands
54, 56

Enterline, Sandra San Francisco, California 389

Esser, Suzanne Amstelveen, Netherlands 275

F

Falkenhagen, Diane Galveston, Texas 264

Ferrero, Tom Windsor, Connecticut 343

Fetter, Peg St. Louis, Missouri 41

Field-Sloan, McIrvin Salem, New York 244

Fisch, Arline San Diego, California 304

Fitzgerald, Lilly Spencer, Massachusetts 147

Fleischhut, Jantje Amsterdam, Netherlands 50, 116, 320, 326, 379

Fly, Karen Copenhagen, Denmark 312

Flynn, Pat High Falls, New York 293

Ford, Steven Philadelphia, Pennsylvania 124

Forlano, David Philadelphia, Pennsylvania 124

Forsbrook, Gill Ely, United Kingdom 181

Freda, David C. San Clemente, California 169

Frias, Javier Moreno Idar-Oberstein, Germany 241

Friedlich, Donald Madison, Wisconsin 67

Fritsch, Karl Island Bay, New Zealand 10, 130, 140

Funaki, Mari Carlton, Australia 285, 394

G

Galandiuk, Markian Memphis, Tennessee 308

Gamisch, Hagen Sipplingen, Germany 332

Gardner, Glynis Lansdowne, New Zealand 301

Gilbertson, Catherine Clark Caddington, United Kingdom 44

Giles, Geoffrey D. Asheville, North Carolina 90, 233

Glebe, Wesley State College, Pennsylvania 209

Glik, Moritz New York, New York 135

Gollberg, Joanna Asheville, North Carolina 278

Good, Michael Rockport, Maine 148

Gore, Caroline Kalamazoo, Michigan 74

Gralnick, Lisa Madison, Wisconsin 49

Graziano, Visintin Padova, Italy 394

Grov, Kirsti Reinsborg Oslo, Norway 305

Gurhan New York, New York 135

H

Hafermalz-Wheeler, Christine Waiheke Island, New Zealand 347

Haga, Lee Rumsey Portland, Oregon 354

Hanevold, Ingjerd Asker, Norway 367

Hannon, Rebecca Ithaca, New York 65, 178, 370

Hansen, Castello Grevie, Sweden 313

Hash, Arthur David New Paltz, New York 183

Heald, Betty Santa Fe, New Mexico 119, 353

Hedman, Hanna Stockholm, Sweden 295

Heerkens, Ineke Amsterdam, Netherlands 298

Heindl, Anna Vienna, Austria 83

Heinrich, Barbara Pittsford, New York 144, 348, 351

Herman, Thomas Stone Ridge, New York 350

Herynek, Pavel Olomouc, Czech Republic 374

Higashi, April Berkeley, California 273

Hill, Thomas San Francisco, California 329

Hiller, Mirjam Potsdam, Germany 311, 363

Hipólito, Leonor Lisbon, Portugal 359

Hiraiwa, Tomoyo Tokyo, Japan 36

Holmes, Mike San Francisco, California 247

Hoogeboom, Peter Amsterdam, Netherlands 238, 366

Hu, Mary Lee Seattle, Washington 344, 397

Hunter, Marianne Rancho Palos Verdes, California 349

I

Imperia, Giovanna Katy, Texas 109

Inglis, Kath Underdale, Australia 114

Irick, Chris Utica, New York 37

Ishikawa, Mari Munich, Germany 64

Ishiyama, Reiko New York, New York 227

J

Jackson, Rob Athens, Georgia 230

Jacquard, Nicole Bloomington, Indiana 26, 310

Jendis, Stephanie Berlin, Germany 141

Jivetin, Sergey High Falls, New York 382

Jocz, Daniel Cambridge, Massachusetts 271

John, Svenja Berlin, Germany 8, 115, 143, 315

Jung, Jun Won San Ju City, Korea 296

Jünger, Hermann Zorneding ot Poering, Germany 280

K

Kalman, Lauren Cleveland Heights, Ohio 137

Kamata, Jiro Munich, Germany 262, 287, 316

Kang, Yeonmi Seoul, Korea 204

Kanner, Dahlia Kingston, Rhode Island 33

Katsari, Rallou Athens, Greece 43

Kellogg, Jennifer Brooklyn, New York 53

Kerman, Janis Westmount, Canada 233

Kessler, Beppe Amsterdam, Netherlands 274

Keyes, Lanelle W. Savannah, Georgia 283

Kiffer, Christo Little Rock, Arkansas 14

Kim, Hye Won Seoul, Korea 203

Kivarkis, Anya Eugene, Oregon 155

Klakulak, Lisa Asheville, North Carolina 175

Klemm, Susanne Amsterdam, Netherlands 122, 358, 360

Klockmann, Beate Amsterdam, Netherlands 40, 163, 364

Kodré, Helfried Vienna, Austria 226

Koh, Hee-Seung Deokyang-ku, Korea 96

Kolb, Jocelyn Parkesburg, Pennsylvania 198

Krakowski, Yael Vernon, Canada 191

Krinos, Daphne London, United Kingdom 318

Kruger, Daniel Berlin, Germany 171, 272

Kuebeck, Andrew L. Bloomington, Indiana 211

Künnap, Julia Maria Tallinn, Estonia 373

Künzli, Otto Munich, Germany 54, 55, 302, 316

L

Lahover, Shay Tel Aviv, Israel 325

Laken, Birgit Haarlem, Netherlands 371

LaPlantz, David Santa Fe, New Mexico 196

Lee, Seung-Hea Providence, Rhode Island 235

Lee, Seung Jin Seoul, Korea 105

Lehmann, Nicole Halle, Germany 258

Lewis, Keith A. Thorp, Washington 93

Lewton-Brain, Charles Calgary, Canada 199

Lilot, Kim Eric San Francisco, California 21

Lim, Cesar Beverly Hills, California 12

Linssen, Nel Nymegen, Netherlands 25

Logan, Terri Richmond, Indiana 352

Lorenz, Dieter Idar-Oberstein, Germany 392

Lozier, Deborah Oakland, California 215

Lühtje, Christa Stockdorf, Germany 393

Lumsden, Ann L. Ottawa, Canada 127

Luttin, Sim Clifton Hill, Australia 340

M

MacBain, Kenneth C. Morristown, New Jersey 118

Macdonald, Marcia A. Eugene, Oregon 27, 248

MacNeil, Linda Kensington, New Hampshire 229

Maierhofer, Fritz, Vienna, Austria 271

Mälk, Kadri Tallinn, Estonia 85

Mann, Thomas New Orleans, Louisiana 115

Mapp, Owen Paraparaumu, New Zealand 20

Marchetti, Stefano Padova, Italy 42, 277, 346

Marsland, Sally Melbourne, Australia 193

Martin-Cust, Robin Stonington, Maine 228

Maruyama, Sora Tokyo, Japan 57

Matheis, Julie A. Haiku, Hawaii 165

Mathes, Jesse Golden, Colorado 19

Matsunaga, Tomomi Kyoto, Japan 242

Matthews, Leslie Adelaide, Australia 35, 333

May, Susan London, United Kingdom 239

McAllister, Wendy Stevenson, Maryland 218

McCreary, Karen Long Beach, California 118

McCreight, Tim Brunswick, Maine 182

Mei-Fang, Jiang Tainan, Taiwan 5, 376

Melland, Nanna Oslo, Norway 331

Metcalf, Bruce Bala Cynwyd, Pennsylvania 197, 249

Milheiro, Teresa Lisboa, Portugal 104

Moje, Mascha Baladava, Australia 336

Morel, Sonia Lausanne, Switzerland 87

Morrison, Jessica Newport, Australia 129

Moty, Eleanor Tucson, Arizona 348

Muir, Tom Perrysburg, Ohio 102

Munsteiner, Tom Stipshausen, Germany 48

N

Nervous System (Jessica Rosenkrantz and Jesse Louis-Rosenberg) Shutesbury, Massachusetts 86

Neubauer, Ben Portland, Oregon 76

Nikolopoulou, Poly Athens, Greece 330

Norrman, Charlotta Årsta, Sweden 92

Norton, Shelley Hamilton, New Zealand 172

Noten, Atelier Ted Amsterdam, Netherlands 330

Nuell, Mark London, United Kingdom 136

Nÿland, Evert Amsterdam, Netherlands 111

O

Oh, Miwha Concord, Massachusetts 42

Onodera, Masako Bowling Green, Ohio 321

Oppermann, Laurence Lyon, France 72

oye, emiko San Francisco, California 263

P

Paganin, Barbara Venice, Italy 368

Pankowski, Gina Seattle, Washington 46

Papac, Seth Everett, Washington 70

Park, Sujin Glen Cove, New York 309

Passi, Seainin Belfast, United Kingdom 13

Paxon, Adam Keswick, United Kingdom 31

Pearse, Mary Hallam Athens, Georgia 377

Pellegrini, Maria P. Florence, Italy 362

Perkins, Sarah Springfield, Missouri 62

Peters, Ruudt Amsterdam, Netherlands 177, 274

Phillips, Maria Seattle, Washington 168

Pierce, Shari Munich, Germany 160

Pinchuk, Anya Washington, D.C. 217, 388

Pinchuk, Natalya Pittsburgh, Pennsylvania 212

Ploof, Chris Pawtucket, Rhode Island 398

Preston, Mary Mamaroneck, New York 155

Price, Beverly Johannesburg, South Africa 314

Priest, Linda Kindler Bedford, Massachusetts 23

Prindiville, Kathleen R. Warren, Rhode Island 254

Prins, Katja Amsterdam, Netherlands 372

R

Raible, Kent Nevada City, California 401

Rath, Tina Portland, Maine 216

Redman, Jayne Portland, Maine 290

Reed, Todd Boulder, Colorado 223, 232, 400

Revere, Alan San Francisco, California 45

Rezac, Suzan Oak Park, Illinois 221

Richter, Sybille Weimar, Germany 188

Rickard, Tessa E. Hamtramck, Michigan 84

Ritchie, Pamela Halifax, Canada 32

Roberts, Brian Pella, Iowa 252

Rossi, Marzia Florence, Italy 114

Rothmann, Gerd Munich, Germany 375

Rust, Vina Seattle, Washington 158

Ryan, Elizabeth Easthampton, Massachusetts 113

Ryan, Jacqueline Todi, Italy 15, 47, 150, 338, 339, 390

S

Saito, Kayo Ramsgate, United Kingdom 378

Sajet, Philip Latour de France, France 77, 161

Samuels, Vanessa Sydney, Australia 239

Sawyer, George Minneapolis, Minnesota 149

Schick, Marjorie Pittsburg, Kansas 11, 91

Schmid, Monica Castro Valley, California 185

Schmitz, Claude Luxembourg 202

Schneider, Mark Long Beach, California 133

Schobinger, Bernhard Richterswil, Switzerland 259

Schutz, Biba New York, New York 292

Semeraro, Alessia Aiello, Italy 189, 370

Sepkus, Alex New York, New York 146

Seufert, Karin Berlin, Germany 323, 337

Sherman, Sondra San Diego, California 18

Shiga, Kristin Mitsu Portland, Oregon 250

Shimizu, Yoko Florence, Italy 224, 225

Simon, Marjorie Philadelphia, Pennsylvania 219

Slemmons, Kiff Chicago, Illinois 69

Sloan, Susan Kasson Hillsdale, New Jersey 319

Smith, Jan Salt Spring Island, Canada 355

Smith, Lulu Seattle, Washington 139

Smulovitz, Anika Boise, Idaho 66

Song, Jay Savannah, Georgia 220, 260

Sonia, Yael New York, New York 132

Sonobe, Etsuko Yamanashi, Japan 58, 78

Speckner, Bettina Ubersee, Germany 75

Stach, Gisbert Graefelfing, Germany 55

Stanionis, Lin Overbrook, Kansas 297

Steepy, Tracy Providence, Rhode Island 286

Strzelec, Rebecca Altoona, Pennsylvania 59

Sugawara, Noriko New York, New York 146

Swol, Carol-lynn DeKalb, Illinois 174, 322

T

Talcott, Lori Seattle, Washington 153

Tammaro, Anthony Carshohocken, Pennsylvania 237

Thakker, Salima Wuustwezel, Belgium 279

Thibado, Ken Utica, New York 102

Thiewes, Rachelle El Paso, Texas 381

Toops, Cynthia Seattle, Washington 97, 267

Trask, Jennifer High Falls, New York 164

Tridenti, Fabrizio Vasto, Italy 95

Tryon, Loretta Coopersburg, Pennsylvania 184

Tsao, Ting-Ting Tainan, Taiwan 266

Turner, Julia San Francisco, California 73, 265

U

Uli Amsterdam, Netherlands 317

V

Vági, Flóra Budapest, Hungary 246

Valdma, Maria Tallinn, Estonia 94

Van Aswegen, Johan Providence, Rhode Island 71

van der Donk, Jacomijn Amsterdam, Netherlands 64

van der Laan, Christel Kallaroo, Australia 51, 68, 120

van der Leest, Felieke Øystest, Norway 24, 173, 253, 328, 365, 380

Vancza, Veleta High Falls, New York 341

Vandamme, Ingeborg Amsterdam, Netherlands 112

VannAusdle, Garry Charlottesville, Virginia 145

Verbeek, Miriam El Zutphen, Netherlands 108

Vilanova, Estela Saez Amsterdam, Netherlands 214

Vilhena, Manuel Estoril, Portugal 58, 194

Von Dohnanyi, Babette Hamburg, Germany 138

W

Wagner, Andrea Amsterdam, Netherlands 107

Wardill, Kathryn Melbourne, Australia 356

Way, Karla Fitzroy, Australia 243

Weaver, Scott Elmira, New York 282

Weaver, Sean Elmira, New York 282

Weber, Norman Aufkirch, Germany 225

Wehrens, Jan Munich, Germany 334

White, Heather West Roxbury, Massachusetts 22

Willemstijn, Francis Wormerveer, Netherlands 81

Williamson, David Berea, Ohio 99

Williamson, Roberta Berea, Ohio 99

Winter, Jasmin Hamburg, Germany 281

Wise, Jeff Durango, Colorado 210

Wise, Susan Durango, Colorado 210

Woodford, Lawrence Halifax, Canada 387

Y

Yamada, Mizuko Toyko, Japan 187

Yen, Liaung Chung Henrietta, New York 126, 151

Yokouchi, Sayumi Brooklyn, New York 159

Yuksek, Yesim Istanbul, Turkey 134

Yung, Lily Toronto, Canada 386

Z

Zanella, Annamaria Padova, Italy 82, 346

Zettle-Sterling, Renee Coopersville, Michigan 300

Zobel, Michael Konstanz, Germany 16, 402

Zorzi, Alberto Padova, Italy 78